TINY TOTS

TIMBERDOODLE'S CURRICULUM HANDBOOK

2018-2019 EDITION

"HEDGEHOG" COVER ART BY TESSA AGE 7
"MOON, STARS, HEARTS" COVER ART BY REBECCA G. AGE 14
ALL THE AMAZING INTERIOR DOODLES PROVIDED BY OUR TALENTED CUSTOMERS

©2018 Timberdoodle Company

All rights reserved. Photocopying and digital reproduction permitted by and for use of the original purchasing family only.

WE'RE SO GLAD YOU'RE HERE!

Congratulations on choosing to homeschool this year! Whether this is your first year as a teacher or your tenth, we're confident you'll find that there is very little that compares to watching your child's learning take off. In fact, teaching can be quite addictive, so be forewarned!

ON YOUR MARK, GET SET, GO!

Preparing for your first "school day" is very easy. Peruse this guide, look over the typical schedule, browse the introductions in your books, and you will be ready to go.

GET SUPPORT

Are you looking for a place to hang out online with like-minded homeschoolers? Do you wonder how someone else handled a particular science kit? Or do you wish you could encourage someone who is just getting started this year? Join one or more of our Facebook groups.

Timberdoodlers of all ages:
https://www.facebook.com/groups/Timberdoodle/

Timberdoodlers with tiny tots — kindergarten students:
www.facebook.com/groups/EarlyTimberdoodle

Timberdoodlers using Non-religious kits:
https://www.facebook.com/groups/SecularTimberdoodle

SCHEDULE CUSTOMIZER

Your 2018-2019 Tiny Tots Curriculum Kit includes access to our Schedule Customizer, where you can not only adjust the school weeks, but also tweak the checklist to include exactly what you want on your schedule. To get started, just click the link in your access email and visit the scheduling website!
www.TimberdoodleSchedules.com

If you ordered through a charter school or don't have that link for some other reason, just email schedules@Timberdoodle.com and we'll get that sorted out ASAP. (Including your order number will really speed that process up for you.)

WE WILL HELP

We would love to assist you if questions come up, so please don't hesitate to contact us with any questions, comments, or concerns. Whether you contact us by phone, email, or live online chat, you will get a real person who is eager to serve you and your family.

YOU WILL LOVE THIS!

This year you and your student will learn more than you hoped while having a blast. Ready? Have an absolutely amazing year!

CONTENTS

07   MEET YOUR HANDBOOK
08   YOU'RE GOING TO LOVE THIS
10   PLANNING
16   NEWBORN - 3 MONTHS
26   4-6 MONTHS
36   7-9 MONTHS
46   10-12 MONTHS
56   13-16 MONTHS
66   17-20 MONTHS
74   21-24 MONTHS
84   READING CHALLENGE
92   LEARNING TOGETHER
93   ACTIVE BABY... CHECKLISTS

98   VISUAL & VERBAL SKILLS
105 MOTOR SKILLS
114 STEM
119 SOCIAL SKILLS
124 SENSORY
130 DEVELOPMENTAL PLAY
135 CONVERGENT & DIVERGENT THINKING
136 HOMESCHOOLING YOUR BABY — LEARNING STYLES
138 HOMESCHOOLING YOUR BABY — ENVIRONMENT
140 TODDLER CONTAINMENT 101

MEET YOUR HANDBOOK
THREE QUICK TIPS TO GET YOU STARTED

All the Details Included
This Timberdoodle Curriculum Kit is available in three different standard levels. The Infant Kit features items most utilized by ages 0-12 months. The Toddler Kit includes the items most used for 12 through 24-month-olds. The Tiny Tots Kit includes all the components for 0-24 months. In this guide, you'll find an overview and any tips for each of the items included in the Tiny Tots Elite Curriculum Kit. If you purchased an Infant or Toddler Kit, or if you customized your kit, you chose not to receive every item, so you'll only need to familiarize yourself with the products which were included in your kit.

Simple Is Better
We really believe that, so your guide is as simple as we could make it. First up are the annual planner and sample weekly checklists, the absolute backbones of Timberdoodle's Curriculum Kits. More on those in a moment. Next up are short bios of each item in your kit, ideal for refreshing your memory on why each is included, or to show off exactly what you will be focusing on with your little one this year. We've also thrown in our tips or tricks to make this year more awesome for all of you. Finally, we'll conclude with our favorite articles and tidbits amassed in our nearly-35-years of homeschool experience.

Why Week by Week Works
We know you. OK, maybe not you personally, but we have yet to meet a homeschooler who doesn't have other irons in the fire. From homesteading or running a business to swimming lessons or doctor's appointments, your weeks are not dull. A daily schedule could overwhelm you both, but having a weekly checklist is the perfect blend of enough structure to finish in a timely fashion and enough freedom that your adventures won't make for stressful catch-up days. Relax; this is so doable!

YOU'RE GOING TO LOVE THIS!

Newborn to 24 months is a huge developmental range to cover in a single curriculum set, especially when you consider how much your child changes and grows during this time. For this kit we have included our most invaluable, unusual, and versatile materials, designed to grow with your baby. Once he has mastered these tools, he is ready for the preschool set, even if he isn't yet over 24 months. (By the same token, some two-year-olds will be best served by spending more time with these tools, so don't rush your toddler into preschool, either!)

Planning
Your goal is to pace your baby so that he is constantly learning, but not overwhelmed. Our family likes to use a weekly check-off sheet so that nothing gets lost in the shuffle. Print it from the online scheduler so that you can modify it for your child, or photocopy the appropriate page in this guide.

What Is the Goal Here?
We aren't interested in producing the smartest baby in the world for the sake of bragging, or "trick-training" a little one just to prove we can. Instead, our goal is to give you tools and ideas of things you can do with your baby to not only stimulate him mentally and physically, but also develop more and more of a relationship (attachment/bonding), and to maximize his strengths. Since your baby is wired to learn, the question is not whether you will teach him, but what you will teach, and how deliberately you will go about it.

Character First
Another thing to keep in mind is that, more than educating your baby, you are teaching this little one how to learn. Build his attention span little by little. Encourage perseverance when he wants to fling the pieces across the floor. Feed his curiosity for all things moving. Reward hard work, encourage language development, and expect obedience as he matures. These are more than just life skills–they are part of character development, and as such are much more important than any academic skill.

Reading Second
Make it your goal to spend some time reading with your baby every day. We have included several books in your kit to get you started, but please don't think that they are truly enough. Supplement them with books from your library or your family's own collection. Regardless of what you choose to read, make it part of your daily routine to sit down and read together. Not only does this develop his own appetite for reading, but it is an incredible tool for building vocabulary and budding language skills.

Siblings
If your baby is blessed with older siblings, keep them involved in his education. Not only will he have more opportunities to learn, but the siblings will learn the invaluable skill of teaching. We suggest going over the weekly chart and highlighting the things you'd like them to do. For instance, everything highlighted yellow is for big brother to do, and the ones in green are reserved for big sister. Then let them check the work off as they go. Baby will love it, they will be delighted with their accomplishments, and you just might get a moment to plan tonight's menu!

PLANNING YOUR YEAR

HOW TO USE TIMBERDOODLE'S PLANNERS

Make This Work for You
In all of the chaos of caring for and feeding a tiny one, we find ourselves asking: Did we do the puzzle twice this week, or was it last week? And when was the last time baby actually had tummy time? To make your life easier, we've included easy weekly checklists. You'll be able to see at a glance that you really haven't tackled sensory play yet this week, but you've done motor skills three times already. As always, capitalize on your own and your baby's interests every week, and don't be tied to a script. But we think you'll find the at-a-glance ideas to still be helpful and freeing.

Use the Customizer
On the next pages you'll find sample weekly checklists for Infant, Toddler, and the complete Tiny Tots kit. Before you photocopy them, though, take a moment to check out the custom schedule builder that came free with your kit. You'll not only easily adjust the weeks, but also tweak the checklist to include exactly what you want listed at www.TimberdoodleSchedules.com. Not sure why you'd want to do that? Check out our case studies beginning on page 16.

Designed for Maximum Flexibility
No two families are identical, so don't expect your pace or daily school time to be identical. Are you off to the dentist's this week? You won't fall behind by taking a day off. Or perhaps you'd like to save the most travel-friendly tools for the big trip this weekend. That's not a problem!

Find Your Normal
We asked parents who used this kit how long their students spent on "school." They estimated that they spent 3-21 hours a week using the tools in this kit. Of course, this will vary a lot from newborn to late toddler, and from child to child, so make sure you allow yourself and your child some time to find your own rhythm!

Active Baby, Healthy Brain
If you can only do one part of this kit, please make it this book. It covers so much! To make implementing it easier, we've added Active Baby checklists on pages 93-97.

Our Babies
In addition to the five original Timberdoodlers (now grown) in less than two years of foster care we've welcomed 12 tiny ones (so far) into our home under the age of two. From the newborn just discharged from the hospital to the 20-month-old that needed a safe place for a day, each little one has taught us much. The biggest lesson though? Each child is SO different! Along with the starter schedules, we'll be including notes with possible scenarios where you'd want to adjust your plans to boost your child's development. (Just FYI, we won't be using the real names or precise scenarios that we've encountered - even if we have learned a ton from our precious ones!)

We Aren't Going to Talk About This
Your app or parenting book will tell you how many times a day to expect to feed your tiny one, how to swaddle him, and when to anticipate developmental milestones. We're going to leave that for the experts and focus in on our area of expertise - connecting with your child while you grow his brain.

YOUR ANNUAL PLANNER

	CURRICULUM	LESSONS OR PAGES	= PER WEEK
Guide	Active Baby, Healthy Brain	135 exercises	Daily
Visual & Verbal Skills	Indestructibles (set of 4)	4 books	reading: daily
	Day and Night: First Words Book	1 book	tummy time
	Let's Sign, Baby!	1 book	reading: daily
	My First Baby Signs	1 book	reading: daily
	Very First Book of Things to Spot, set of 3	3 books	reading: daily
	ABC Baby Signs	1 book	reading: daily
Motor Skills	The Amazing Peanut Ball	unlimited	as desired
	Bumpie Gertie Ball	unlimited	several times a week
	Caterpillar Stacking	unlimited	1-2x a week
	Haba Palette of Pegs	unlimited	2x a week
	Original Gertie Ball	unlimited	several times a week
	Poke-A-Dot Popper	unlimited	as desired
	Slinky Pop Toobs	unlimited	2x a week
STEM	3-D ShapeSorter	unlimited	3x a week
	Stackable Forest	unlimited	1-2x a week
	Grippies Shakers	unlimited	2x a week
Social Skills	Wimmer - Ferguson Baby Mirror	unlimited	daily
	Making Faces: A First Book of Emotions	1 book	2x a week
	Wee Baby Stella	unlimited	as desired
	Miffy Hide & Seek	unlimited	as desired
Sensory Skills	Starry Night Playsilk	unlimited	as desired
	pipSquigz Loops	unlimited	as desired
	Taggies Crinkle Heather Hedgehog	unlimited	as desired
	Yoee Baby Fox	unlimited	daily
	Tactile Search and Match	unlimited	as desired
Developmental Play	Bolli Teether	unlimited	as desired
	Amber and Wood Teething Ring	unlimited	3-5x a week
	Gertie the Good Goose	unlimited	as desired
	Romeo the Greedy Toad	unlimited	as desired
	Walter Squeaker	unlimited	as desired

WEEK BY WEEK
FLEXIBILITY & FRAMEWORK IN ONE

These weekly checklists are the framework of your week, and they are designed for maximum flexibility. Just check off each item as you get it done for the week and you'll be able to see at a glance that you still need to do __ this week.

A Little Every Day, or All at Once?
At this age, you'll want to spread out topics throughout the week as much as possible. For instance, it will be better for your baby's brain to read together multiple times a week instead of one super-long reading session. Use common sense, though–if you're on a reading roll, don't stop just because "the list" said so!

Week 1 Hints
As you get started this year, realize that you are just getting your sea-legs. Expect your system to take a little longer and be a little less smooth than it will be by the end of the month. As you get your feet under you, you will discover the rhythm that works best for you! If you don't know where to begin each day, why not try starting with something from Active Baby? It will get your child's brain in gear and set a great tone for the rest of the day.

Pro Tip
When you first get out this week's checklist, remember to check off all the things you don't need to do this week. For instance, if your toddler has outgrown the Crinkle Hedgehog, just check it off. Doesn't that feel better?

12   www.timberdoodle.com • ©2018

WEEKLY CHECKLIST (INFANT KIT)

Category	Item	Frequency						
Guide	Active Baby, Healthy Brain	daily						
Visual & Verbal Skills	Reading: Indestructibles (set of 4), Day and Night: First Words Book	daily						
Visual & Verbal Skills	Sign Language: Let's Sign, Baby!; My First Baby Signs	daily						
Motor Skills	The Amazing Peanut Ball	daily						
Motor Skills	Bumpie Gertie Ball	3x a week						
Social Skills	Wimmer - Ferguson Baby Mirror	daily						
Sensory Skills	Yoee Baby Fox	daily						
Sensory Skills	Starry Night Playsilk	2x a week						
Sensory Skills	pipSquigz Loops	2x a week						
Sensory Skills	Taggies Crinkle Heather Hedgehog	as desired						
Developmental Play	Teethers and Tools: Bolli Teether, Amber and Wood Teething Ring, Gertie the Good Goose	as desired						
Developmental Play	Romeo the Greedy Toad	1-2x a week						
Developmental Play	Walter Squeaker	1-2x a week						

Weekly Checklist (Toddler Kit)

Category	Item	Frequency					
Guide	Active Baby, Healthy Brain	daily					
Visual & Verbal Skills	Reading: Very First Books of Things to Spot set	daily					
Visual & Verbal Skills	Sign Language: ABC Baby Signs	daily					
Motor Skills	Gertie Ball	3x a week					
Motor Skills	Caterpillar Stacking	1-2x a week					
Motor Skills	Haba Palette of Pegs	2x a week					
Motor Skills	Poke-A-Dot Popper	2x a week					
Motor Skills	Slinky Pop Toobs	2x a week					
STEM	3-D ShapeSorter	3x a week					
STEM	Stackable Forest	1-2x a week					
STEM	Grippies Shakers	2x a week					
Social Skills	Making Faces: A First Book of Emotions	2x a week					
Social Skills	Wee Baby Stella	2x a week					
Social Skills	Miffy Hide & Seek	2x a week					
Sensory Skills	Tactile Search and Match	2x a week					

WEEKLY CHECKLIST (TINY TOTS/ELITE)

Category	Item	Frequency						
Guide	Active Baby, Healthy Brain	daily						
Visual & Verbal Skills	Reading: Indestructibles (set of 4), Day and Night: First Words Book, Very First Books of Things to Spot	daily						
	Sign Language: Let's Sign, Baby!; My First Baby Signs; ABC Baby Signs	daily						
Motor Skills	The Amazing Peanut Ball	daily						
	Gertie Balls	3x a week						
	Caterpillar Stacking	1-2x a week						
	Haba Palette of Pegs	2x a week						
	Poke-A-Dot Popper	2x a week						
	Slinky Pop Toobs	2x a week						
STEM	3-D ShapeSorter	3x a week						
	Stackable Forest	1-2x a week						
	Grippies Shakers	2x a week						
Social Skills	Wimmer - Ferguson Baby Mirror	daily						
	Making Faces: A First Book of Emotions	2x a week						
	Wee Baby Stella	2x a week						
	Miffy Hide & Seek	2x a week						
Sensory Skills	Starry Night Playsilk	2x a week						
	pipSquigz Loops	2x a week						
	Taggies Crinkle Heather Hedgehog	as desired						
	Yoee Baby Fox	daily						
	Tactile Search and Match	2x a week						
Developmental Play	Teethers and Tools: Bolli Teether, Amber and Wood Teething Ring, Gertie the Good Goose	as desired						
	Romeo the Greedy Toad	1-2x a week						
	Walter Squeaker	1-2x a week						

NEWBORN THROUGH 3 MONTHS

CUDDLING AND NURTURING FOR BRAIN DEVELOPMENT

Every Touch Grows His Brain

Recent studies are proving again and again that the single most impactful thing you can do for your newborn's development is to pick him up. Holding him helps him regulate his system and, in ways they are still defining, strengthens his neural network. What does this mean for you? Well, if he has a fussy day and you are barely able to set him down long enough to use the bathroom, let alone enough to get through his list - don't worry! You're already doing the most important thing.

Set These Things Aside

We don't expect any newborn through three-month-olds to be signing, so the sign language books are either used for general reading or set aside for now. Romeo the Greedy Toad and pipSquigz Loops are also a bit much for this age. Frankly it's a little premature to even have the teethers here, but by the time your baby is three months old, he'll likely be ready to grasp some of them.

Reading

Yes, it seems a little ridiculous to read with someone who can't even focus their eyes, but this really is critical! Reading increases auditory processing skills, visual perception, language development, connection, and so much more. Read a book from your kit, or the library, or your bookshelf... content matters little at this stage; what you're looking for is the experience.

Sensory Input

Yoee Baby should come out to play every day. The frequent exposure helps him learn to process sensations all over his body, while also helping with bonding and so much more. The Playsilk and Bumpie Gertie Ball may be used in the same fashion, by gently rubbing/brushing/rolling on his skin. Add as many other gentle textures as you can and watch his brain grow!

Auditory Processing

Any of these tools (or the ones you already own) that have a sound to them may be used for auditory processing. Simply rattle or squeak them where your child has to turn his head slightly to see them. As his skills improve, you'll be able to place them farther away and squeak/rattle them less before he focuses on them.

Wear Your Baby

If you have the opportunity to wear your baby, do so! Not only will he be soothed and regulated by your presence and touch, but he will also receive much-needed vestibular input all day long as you move throughout your day. And don't get us started on the auditory, visual, and connection advantages!

Case #1: Elias

Sweet baby Elias is 2-weeks-old, and was discharged from the NICU today. You notice that he is very "jumpy" to any sounds and cries at even gentle touches.

In addition to cuddling and wearing him as much as possible, you'll also want to emphasize as much sensory input as possible. Touch him softly, with warm hands, as often as possible. Consider parking Yoee Baby and your favorite lotion at the changing table. After each change (or every other) strip him down to his diaper and stroke/lotion him while singing/talking to him. Use the auditory tools in your toolbox (rattles, squeakers, etc.) to help him become less and less startled by common sounds.

Case #2: Piper
At three months, you notice that Piper really lacks muscle strength. She cries during tummy time and melts into you when you hold her.

For Piper you're going to want to emphasize all things gross motor as much as you can. Revisit your Active Baby, Healthy Brain checklist and buckle down to complete as much of the chart as possible each week. Try putting her mirror at the changing table (hey, we know you'll be hanging out there a lot!) and having her be on her stomach for exactly 1 minute after each diaper change. When that is achievable without stressing her out, increase it to two minutes, etc. Soon you'll be able to move her to the floor without making her cry!

Case #3: Ranger
Tiny Ranger is a month old, but still in newborn clothes and with noted drug exposure. He cries a lot and seems very stiff with frantic, jerky motions.

Ranger needs help regulating his body. (Swaddling, while not a point of our kit, is worth noting, as it's hugely helpful!) For him,

you will likely be modifying many of the sensory activities. You want it to almost be too much for him, but never to cross that line.

Newborns and tiny ones usually start sneezing/coughing/yawning when they are beginning to be stressed. (Of course, they also do all these things for normal physiological reasons too!) If you find that putting on lotion makes him frantic, try warming your hands under hot water first, slowing your motions, etc. You want his abilities to be growing without adding more stress to his life, especially since much of his life is going to taken up with just getting calories in him right now.

For some babies, the cuddling/rocking/swaying/singing that we instinctively do to help them calm down is in itself distressing. (This is particularly true of drug-exposed infants or babies with a lot of NICU time.) If he becomes extremely overwrought, try swaddling him, giving him a pacifier and setting him in his crib in a quiet, dark room, minimizing the sensory input he's receiving. As he calms down, pick him up and keep him at arm's length, drawing him to yourself as he allows.

In calm times, work on rocking him gently until he begins to show the earliest signs of stress, then stop. Slowly but surely, you're re-wiring his brain!

0-3 Month Weekly Checklist

Category	Item	Frequency						
Guide	Active Baby, Healthy Brain	daily						
Visual & Verbal Skills	Reading: Indestructibles (set of 4); Day and Night: First Words Book; Let's Sign, Baby!; My First Baby Signs	daily						
Motor Skills	The Amazing Peanut Ball	daily						
Motor Skills	Bumpie Gertie Ball	3x a week						
Social Skills	Wimmer - Ferguson Baby Mirror	daily						
Sensory Skills	Yoee Baby Fox	daily						
Sensory Skills	Starry Night Playsilk	2x a week						
Sensory Skills	Taggies Crinkle Heather Hedgehog	as desired						
Developmental Play	Teethers and Tools: Bolli Teether, Amber and Wood Teething Ring, Gertie the Good Goose	as desired						
Developmental Play	Walter Squeaker	1-2x a week						

ACTIVE BABY... 0-3 MONTHS

	ACTIVITY (+ AGE IF NOTED)	MON.	TUES.	WEDS.	THURS.	FRI.
Basic Exercises	Slowly massage front & back					
	Tummy time (5 days+)					
	Leg flexing (2-3 months+)					
	Rocking sideways					
	Gentle turnovers					
	Arm movements					
	Back pushaways					
	Tummy time over a roll					
	Tummy pushaways (4 weeks+)					
	Rolling (2 months+)					
	Feet & leg reflexes (2 months+)					
	Neck & back strengthening (2 months+)					
	Rocking forward (parachute reflex)					
	Hitting/kicking a hanging balloon (2 months+)					
Vestibular Stimulation	Slightly inflated big ball					
	Seated rocking from side to side					
	Hammock swing					
	Stroller ride on bumpy ground					
	Stand and rock (2 months+)					
	Bobbing up & down (2 months+)					
	Rocking, rolling, bouncing on your knees (2 months+)					
	Rocking back and forth (2-3 months+)					
	Rolling on a ball (3 months+)					
	Extreme rocking on your knees (3 months+) 10x					
	"Here We Go Side to Side" (3 months+)					
Music, Rhythm, and Song	Music & nature sounds					
	Stories, rhymes, and "conversations"					
	Dancing (head supported)					
	Bouncing and swaying on his front (4 weeks+)					
	Action rhymes (6 weeks+)					
Vision	Flickering lights (0-2 months) 4x/day					
	Tracking rattle sounds					

"Elias" Sample Weekly Checklist

Guide	Active Baby, Healthy Brain	daily						
Visual & Verbal Skills	Reading: Indestructibles (set of 4); Day and Night: First Words Book; Let's Sign, Baby!; My First Baby Signs	daily						
Motor Skills	The Amazing Peanut Ball	daily						
	Bumpie Gertie Ball	3x a week						
Social Skills	Wimmer - Ferguson Baby Mirror	daily						
Sensory Skills	Yoee Baby Fox	daily						
	Starry Night Playsilk	daily						
	Taggies Crinkle Heather Hedgehog	2x a week						
Developmental Play	Gertie the Good Goose	2x a week						
	Walter Squeaker	1x a week						

Notes

At 2-weeks Elias isn't ready to hold anything and certainly isn't teething, so we removed those teethers from his list.

We also adjusted the x per week so that he is doing auditory exercises with either his Taggie, his Goose, or his Squeaker every day.

The only adjustment we made to Active Baby... was to remove any activity Elias isn't old enough to do yet

"ELIAS" SAMPLE ACTIVE BABY CHECKLIST

	ACTIVITY	MON.	TUES.	WEDS.	THURS.	FRI.
Basic Exercises	Slowly massage front & back					
	Tummy time (5 days+)					
	Rocking sideways					
	Gentle turnovers					
	Arm movements					
	Back pushaways					
	Tummy time over a roll					
	Rocking forward (parachute reflex)					
Vestibular Stimulation	Slightly inflated big ball					
	Seated rocking from side to side					
	Hammock swing					
	Stroller ride on bumpy ground					
Music, Rhythm, and Song	Music & nature sounds					
	Stories, rhymes, and "conversations"					
	Dancing (head supported)					
Vision	Flickering lights (0-2 months) 4x/day					
	Tracking rattle sounds					

"Piper" Sample Weekly Checklist

Guide	Active Baby, Healthy Brain	daily						
Visual & Verbal Skills	Reading: Indestructibles (set of 4); Day and Night: First Words Book; Let's Sign, Baby!; My First Baby Signs	daily						
Motor Skills	The Amazing Peanut Ball	daily						
Motor Skills	Bumpie Gertie Ball	3x a week						
Social Skills	Wimmer - Ferguson Baby Mirror	daily						
Sensory Skills	Yoee Baby Fox	daily						
Sensory Skills	Starry Night Playsilk	1x a week						
Sensory Skills	Taggies Crinkle Heather Hedgehog	1x a week						
Developmental Play	Teethers and Tools: Bolli Teether, Amber and Wood Teething Ring, Gertie the Good Goose	1x a week						
Developmental Play	Walter Squeaker	1x a week						

Notes

Piper is likely ready to hold anything, and may even begin to chew on things this month, so we've left the teethers on her list.

Knowing we really need to work on gross motor skills this month, we minimized almost everything else. However, reading and Yoee Baby are still too important to skip, even during this season of focus.

www.timberdoodle.com • ©2018

"PIPER" SAMPLE ACTIVE BABY CHECKLIST

	ACTIVITY	MON.	TUES.	WEDS.	THURS.	FRI.
Basic Exercises	Slowly massage front & back					
	Tummy time (5 days+)					
	Leg flexing (2-3 months+)					
	Rocking sideways					
	Gentle turnovers					
	Arm movements					
	Back pushaways					
	Tummy time over a roll					
	Tummy pushaways (4 weeks+)					
	Rolling (2 months+)					
	Feet & leg reflexes (2 months+)					
	Neck & back strengthening (2 months+)					
	Rocking forward (parachute reflex)					
	Hitting/kicking a hanging balloon (2 months+)					
Vestibular Stimulation	Slightly inflated big ball					
	Seated rocking from side to side					
	Hammock swing					
	Stroller ride on bumpy ground					
	Stand and rock (2 months+)					
	Bobbing up & down (2 months+)					
	Rocking, rolling, bouncing on your knees (2 months+)					
	Rocking back and forth (2-3 months+)					
	Rolling on a ball (3 months+)					
	Extreme rocking on your knees (3 months+) 10x					
	"Here We Go Side to Side" (3 months+)					
Music, Rhythm, and Song	Music & nature sounds					
	Stories, rhymes, and "conversations"					
	Dancing (head supported)					
	Bouncing and swaying on his front (4 weeks+)					
	Action rhymes (6 weeks+)					
Vision	Tracking rattle sounds					

2018-2019 Tiny Tots Curriculum Handbook • 800.478.0672

"RANGER" SAMPLE WEEKLY CHECKLIST

Guide	Active Baby, Healthy Brain	daily						
Visual & Verbal Skills	Reading: Indestructibles (set of 4); Day and Night: First Words Book; Let's Sign, Baby!; My First Baby Signs	daily						
Motor Skills	The Amazing Peanut Ball	daily						
	Bumpie Gertie Ball	3x a week						
Social Skills	Wimmer - Ferguson Baby Mirror	daily						
Sensory Skills	Yoee Baby Fox	daily						
	Starry Night Playsilk	2x a week						
	Taggies Crinkle Heather Hedgehog	as desired						
Developmental Play	Teethers and Tools: Bolli Teether, Amber and Wood Teething Ring, Gertie the Good Goose	as desired						
	Walter Squeaker	1-2x a week						

Notes

Ranger's schedule looks a lot like Elias' plan. Both little boys need a focus on sensory integration, even though the depth of their need is quite different.

You'll also be tweaking these activities more for Ranger than you would need to for Elias. For instance, Elias may be able to handle a full-volume squeak from Walter at close range, while Ranger is only ready for the tiniest sound at several feet away. Both versions deserve a check off though - you've done what was appropriate for YOUR little one!

	ACTIVITY	MON.	TUES.	WEDS.	THURS.	FRI.
Basic Exercises	Slowly massage front & back					
	Tummy time (5 days+)					
	Rocking sideways					
	Gentle turnovers					
	Arm movements					
	Back pushaways					
	Tummy time over a roll					
	Rocking forward (parachute reflex)					
Vestibular Stimulation	Slightly inflated big ball					
	Seated rocking from side to side					
	Hammock swing					
	Stroller ride on bumpy ground					
Music, Rhythm, and Song	Music & nature sounds					
	Stories, rhymes, and "conversations"					
	Dancing (head supported)					
	Bouncing and swaying on his front (4 weeks+)					
Vision	Flickering lights (0-2 months) 4x/day					
	Tracking rattle sounds					

"RANGER" SAMPLE ACTIVE BABY CHECKLIST

4-6 Months
BECOMING AWARE OF EVERYTHING

To Sign or Not to Sign
At this age your baby is probably not quite ready to sign. However, it is a wonderful stage to begin introducing the concept and modeling it for him. The books are a perfect starting point for that.

Set These Things Aside
Romeo the Greedy Toad is a bit much for this age. You will want to bring out the teethers though! You may or may not want to pull out pipSquigz now. While it will be some time before your baby gets the full advantage of the suction cups, he is getting old enough to enjoy the rattling, chewing, and novel shape.

Reading
Definitely keep up with the daily reading time. As mentioned before, reading increases auditory processing skills, visual perception, language development, connection, and so much more. Read a book from your kit, or the library, or your bookshelf... content matters little at this stage; what you're looking for is the experience.

Sensory Input
Yoee Baby should still come out to play often. The frequent exposure helps him learn to process sensations all over his body, while also helping with bonding and so much more. The Playsilk and Bumpie Gertie Ball may be used in the same fashion, by gently rubbing/brushing/rolling on his skin. Add as many other gentle textures as you can and watch his brain grow!

Auditory Processing
Any of these tools (or the ones you already own) that have a sound to them may be used for auditory processing. Simply rattle or squeak them where your child has to turn his head to see them. At this age he'll be able to track better and father than he was just a few short months ago.

Case #1: Violet
4-month-old Violet is so easy-going and happy that she's kind of baby that makes other parents jealous. However, you wonder if she's "too easy" since she seems quite content to just lie back and watch the action.

Violet is every parent's dream baby, so on one hand, we want to encourage you to relax and soak up these moments, all of them! On the other hand, we want to encourage you to make sure that her easy-going temperament isn't masking low-muscle tone or any disinterest in the world around her. You're going to want to emphasize gross-motor skills for her and monitor her development to make sure all seems well. But you're also going to want to treasure the sweet delight that she is!

Case #2: Santiago
Busy Santiago was born with a club foot and must wear his brace 23 hours a day. He doesn't seem to mind, but at 6 months old he is a bit behind his peers in gross motor skills.

The brace makes Santiago a little more challenging for you to carry/set in certain seats. With a little accommodation and attention though, you'll find that he is still able to be a part of most adventures.

You are going to want to keep a particular eye on his vestibular development, as the temptation will be to set him down more than a "free and clear" baby. His access to sensory activities will also be more limited with the brace in place. Ideally you'll be able to use his hour off each day to not only bathe him but also get him some of that sensory input especially to his feet. Perhaps you could grab the Yoee Baby, Playsilk, and Bumpie Gertie and do some fun foot massages right after his bath?

Case #3: Jade
Sadly, 5- month-old baby Jade has suffered some severe brain damage in her life. Whether this was because of a stroke, shaken baby syndrome, or some other trauma, this is definitely going to impact her development.

The wonderful thing is that infants are wired to have rapidly developing brains even if they have been damaged. You will want to capitalize on this by investing as much time and energy as possible into Jade. Adjust the exercises as much as she needs to make them doable for her.

One note: Often infants with trauma need extra sleep to help their brains heal. If this is the case for Jade, do what you can to help her get all the rest she needs. It will be as important to her as her waking hours are!

4-6 Month Weekly Checklist

Category	Item	Frequency						
Guide	Active Baby, Healthy Brain	daily						
Visual & Verbal Skills	Reading: Indestructibles (set of 4), Day and Night: First Words Book	daily						
	Sign Language: Let's Sign, Baby!; My First Baby Signs	daily						
Motor Skills	The Amazing Peanut Ball	daily						
	Bumpie Gertie Ball	3x a week						
Social Skills	Wimmer - Ferguson Baby Mirror	daily						
Sensory Skills	Yoee Baby Fox	daily						
	Starry Night Playsilk	2x a week						
	pipSquigz Loops	2x a week						
	Taggies Crinkle Heather Hedgehog	as desired						
Developmental Play	Teethers and Tools: Bolli Teether, Amber and Wood Teething Ring, Gertie the Good Goose	as desired						
	Romeo the Greedy Toad	1-2x a week						
	Walter Squeaker	1-2x a week						

www.timberdoodle.com • ©2018

	ACTIVITY (+ AGE IF NOTED)	MON.	TUES.	WEDS.	THURS.	FR...
Basic Exercises	Slowly massage front & back					
	Tummy time (5 days+)					
	Leg flexing (2-3 months+) Pg 20					
	Rocking sideways Pg. 20					
	Gentle turnovers Pg 21					
	Arm movements Pg 21					
	Back pushaways Pg 21					
	Tummy time over a roll					
	Tummy pushaways (4 weeks+)					
	Rolling (2 months+)					
	Feet & leg reflexes (2 months+)					
	Neck & back strengthening (2 months+)					
	Rocking forward (parachute reflex)					
	Hitting/kicking a hanging balloon (2 months+)					
Upper Body	Pull-ups (3 months+)					
	Push-ups (3 months+)					
Vestibular Stimulation	Slightly inflated big ball					
	Seated rocking from side to side					
	Hammock swing Pg. 22					
	Stroller ride on bumpy ground					
	Stand and rock (2 months+)					
	Bobbing up & down (2 months+)					
	Rocking, rolling, bouncing on your knees (2 months+)					
	Rocking back and forth (2-3 months+)					
	Rolling on a ball (3 months+)					
	Extreme rocking on your knees (3 months+) 10x					
	"Here We Go Side to Side" (3 months+)					
Music, Rhythm, Sounds, and Song	Music & nature sounds					
	Stories, rhymes, and "conversations"					
	Dancing (head supported)					
	Bouncing and swaying on his front (4 weeks+)					
	Action rhymes (6 weeks+)					
	Tracking rattle sounds					

ACTIVE BABY... 4-6

"Violet" Sample Weekly Checklist

Guide	Active Baby, Healthy Brain	daily						
Visual & Verbal Skills	Reading: Indestructibles (set of 4), Day and Night: First Words Book	daily						
	Sign Language: Let's Sign, Baby!; My First Baby Signs	daily						
Motor Skills	The Amazing Peanut Ball	daily						
	Bumpie Gertie Ball	3x a week						
Social Skills	Wimmer - Ferguson Baby Mirror	daily						
Sensory Skills	Yoee Baby Fox	daily						
	Starry Night Playsilk	2x a week						
	pipSquigz Loops	2x a week						
	Taggies Crinkle Heather Hedgehog	as desired						
Developmental Play	Teethers and Tools: Bolli Teether, Amber and Wood Teething Ring, Gertie the Good Goose	as desired						
	Romeo the Greedy Toad	1-2x a week						
	Walter Squeaker	1-2x a week						

Changes

None. She's likely going to do perfectly with the "typical" plan unless delays begin to show up.

"VIOLET" SAMPLE ACTIVE BABY...

	ACTIVITY (+ AGE IF NOTED)	MON.	TUES.	WEDS.	THURS.	FRI.
Basic Exercises	Slowly massage front & back					
	Tummy time (5 days+)					
	Leg flexing (2-3 months+)					
	Rocking sideways					
	Gentle turnovers					
	Arm movements					
	Back pushaways					
	Tummy time over a roll					
	Tummy pushaways (4 weeks+)					
	Rolling (2 months+)					
	Feet & leg reflexes (2 months+)					
	Neck & back strengthening (2 months+)					
	Rocking forward (parachute reflex)					
	Hitting/kicking a hanging balloon (2 months+)					
Upper Body	Pull-ups (3 months+)					
	Push-ups (3 months+)					
Vestibular Stimulation	Slightly inflated big ball					
	Seated rocking from side to side					
	Hammock swing					
	Stroller ride on bumpy ground					
	Stand and rock (2 months+)					
	Bobbing up & down (2 months+)					
	Rocking, rolling, bouncing on your knees (2 months+)					
	Rocking back and forth (2-3 months+)					
	Rolling on a ball (3 months+)					
	Extreme rocking on your knees (3 months+) 10x					
	"Here We Go Side to Side" (3 months+)					
Music, Rhythm, Sounds, and Song	Music & nature sounds					
	Stories, rhymes, and "conversations"					
	Dancing (head supported)					
	Bouncing and swaying on his front (4 weeks+)					
	Action rhymes (6 weeks+)					
	Tracking rattle sounds					

"SANTIAGO" SAMPLE WEEKLY CHECKLIST

Guide	Active Baby, Healthy Brain	daily						
Visual & Verbal Skills	Reading: Indestructibles (set of 4), Day and Night: First Words Book	daily						
	Sign Language: Let's Sign, Baby!; My First Baby Signs	daily						
Motor Skills	The Amazing Peanut Ball	daily						
	Bumpie Gertie Ball	3x a week						
Social Skills	Wimmer - Ferguson Baby Mirror	daily						
Sensory Skills	Yoee Baby Fox	daily						
	Starry Night Playsilk	2x a week						
	pipSquigz Loops	2x a week						
	Taggies Crinkle Heather Hedgehog	as desired						
Developmental Play	Teethers and Tools: Bolli Teether, Amber and Wood Teething Ring, Gertie the Good Goose	as desired						
	Romeo the Greedy Toad	1-2x a week						
	Walter Squeaker	1-2x a week						

Changes

While the charts are identical to the sample ones, you're definitely going to need to modify the exercises to make them all work for him. Some of that will be by moving activities to his brace-free time, others you'll just put his legs in the best possible position and live with the "not quite as pictured in the book" accommodation.

The most useful thing you could probably do for him would be to schedule his hour with free feet to be an hour you would be most likely to get one-on-one time with him - perhaps naptime for everyone else?

32 www.timberdoodle.com • ©2018

"SANTIAGO" SAMPLE ACTIVE BABY...

	ACTIVITY (+ AGE IF NOTED)	MON.	TUES.	WEDS.	THURS.	FRI.
Basic Exercises	Slowly massage front & back					
	Tummy time (5 days+)					
	Leg flexing (2-3 months+)					
	Rocking sideways					
	Gentle turnovers					
	Arm movements					
	Back pushaways					
	Tummy time over a roll					
	Tummy pushaways (4 weeks+)					
	Rolling (2 months+)					
	Feet & leg reflexes (2 months+)					
	Neck & back strengthening (2 months+)					
	Rocking forward (parachute reflex)					
	Hitting/kicking a hanging balloon (2 months+)					
Upper Body	Pull-ups (3 months+)					
	Push-ups (3 months+)					
Vestibular Stimulation	Slightly inflated big ball					
	Seated rocking from side to side					
	Hammock swing					
	Stroller ride on bumpy ground					
	Stand and rock (2 months+)					
	Bobbing up & down (2 months+)					
	Rocking, rolling, bouncing on your knees (2 months+)					
	Rocking back and forth (2-3 months+)					
	Rolling on a ball (3 months+)					
	Extreme rocking on your knees (3 months+) 10x					
	"Here We Go Side to Side" (3 months+)					
Music, Rhythm, Sounds, and Song	Music & nature sounds					
	Stories, rhymes, and "conversations"					
	Dancing (head supported)					
	Bouncing and swaying on his front (4 weeks+)					
	Action rhymes (6 weeks+)					
	Tracking rattle sounds					

2018-2019 Tiny Tots Curriculum Handbook • 800.478.0672

"JADE" SAMPLE WEEKLY CHECKLIST

Category	Item	Frequency						
Guide	Active Baby, Healthy Brain	daily						
Visual & Verbal Skills	Reading: Indestructibles (set of 4), Day and Night: First Words Book	daily						
Motor Skills	The Amazing Peanut Ball	daily						
Motor Skills	Bumpie Gertie Ball	3x a week						
Social Skills	Wimmer - Ferguson Baby Mirror	daily						
Sensory Skills	Yoee Baby Fox	daily						
Sensory Skills	Starry Night Playsilk	2x a week						
Sensory Skills	Taggies Crinkle Heather Hedgehog	as desired						
Developmental Play	Teethers and Tools: Bolli Teether, Amber and Wood Teething Ring, Gertie the Good Goose	as desired						
Developmental Play	Walter Squeaker	1-2x a week						

Changes

With Jade's delays, she is operating at roughly a 2-month-old level physically and developmentally. In light of that, let's eliminate all Active Baby... activities for older babies. We also know she's not ready for sign language, so we removed that from her list, along with Greedy Toad and pipSquigz Loops. This month we want to work hard at the activities she's ready for, while encouraging as much sleep and connection as we can.

"JADE" SAMPLE ACTIVE BABY...

ACTIVITY (+ AGE IF NOTED)	MON.	TUES.	WEDS.	THURS.	FRI.
Basic Exercises					
Slowly massage front & back					
Tummy time (5 days+)					
Leg flexing (2-3 months+)					
Rocking sideways					
Gentle turnovers					
Arm movements					
Back pushaways					
Tummy time over a roll					
Tummy pushaways (4 weeks+)					
Rolling (2 months+)					
Feet & leg reflexes (2 months+)					
Neck & back strengthening (2 months+)					
Rocking forward (parachute reflex)					
Hitting/kicking a hanging balloon (2 months+)					
Vestibular Stimulation					
Slightly inflated big ball					
Seated rocking from side to side					
Hammock swing					
Stroller ride on bumpy ground					
Stand and rock (2 months+)					
Bobbing up & down (2 months+)					
Rocking, rolling, bouncing on your knees (2 months+)					
Rocking back and forth (2-3 months+)					
Music, Rhythm, Sounds, and Song					
Music & nature sounds					
Stories, rhymes, and "conversations"					
Dancing (head supported)					
Bouncing and swaying on his front (4 weeks+)					
Action rhymes (6 weeks+)					
Tracking rattle sounds					

7-9 MONTHS
GETTING BABY ON THE MOVE

Let's Start Signing!
Are you ready to build your child's communication skills? This is going to be so fun! You'll begin by modeling the signs and then immediately help your child copy you. For instance, sign "milk" before feeding him, then take his hand in yours and help him sign it in some fashion. Immediately, give him the milk he was "asking" for. Some babies will pick up on this easily, while for others it will take some time. Expect him to start getting it after a month or two - but don't be shocked if it's shorter or longer.

Set These Things Aside
Nothing! You'll be using everything in your Infant Kit this week.

If You Have the Elite Kit
Your child will likely already get a lot of enjoyment out of these items:

Very First Book of Things to Spot set
Gertie Ball
Making Faces: A First Book of Emotions

You may also find that he's ready for Wee Baby Stella or ABC Baby Signs - but that would be a little more rare.

Reading
Your baby will benefit so much from the daily reading time in this season. As mentioned before, reading increases auditory processing skills, visual perception, language development, connection, and so much more. Read a book from your kit, or the library, or your bookshelf... just make sure you're reading together.

Don't Forget Sensory Input
Yoee Baby should still come out to play often. The frequent exposure helps him learn to process sensations all over his body, while also helping with bonding and so much more. The Playsilk and Bumpie Gertie Ball may be used in the same fashion, by gently rubbing/brushing/rolling on his skin. Add as many other gentle textures as you can and watch his brain grow. Bath time is also a sensory experience for him - watch for splashes!

Case #1: Sebastian
At 8 months old, little Sebastian seems clearly in the genius category - if there is such a thing. He can sign half a dozen words readily and learns new ones rapidly/uses them appropriately. He babbles and nearly forms words. He's also progressed rapidly from crawling to already beginning to walk. You feel like this is the shortest babyhood ever!

First off, congratulations! You're obviously pouring into Sebastian's life, and his abilities showcase that. So, the first thing to do is just keep doing what you're doing!

Secondly, try to take a step back and see what areas he is weak on as compared to the rest of his development. For instance, if all the other just-walking tiny ones in his play group are better at recognizing emotions than he is ("Can you make a sad face Sebastian?"), then let's prioritize that over increasing his strengths only.

At the same time, you do want to capitalize on his strengths. If he's wired like a gymnast, find a safe way for him to climb to his heart's content. Or if he's a born book-lover, invest in trips to the library and hours spent soaking up books together. You want to encourage his giftedness in all areas.

For his checklist, there is no need to stay at an 8-month level. Instead, jump right ahead to 9-12 months since those activities are most appropriate to his skills and abilities.

One note:
Don't be discouraged or deflated if Sebastian becomes more "average" over time. A beauty of home schooling is the ability to customize what he's learning to what he's ready for right now. When his growth curve settles down to a normal pace, simply adjust your expectations accordingly and continue to enjoy your time together.

Case #2: Elle
Elle arrived to your home as a darling 7-month-old with an unfortunate history of severe neglect. She is very content to stay in one spot, and has a giant flat spot on the back of her head. She seems developmentally about 4 months old, despite her chronological age.

As you probably suspected, you will want to adjust Elle's plan to her developmental age - 4 months. You will likely find that in a few weeks she is making unprecedented progress across all fields, so re-evaluate often but start with the 4 month checklists.

You will particularly want to make sure that Elle is spending as little time on her back as possible. Her doctor will advise if she needs a helmet or anything, but if you limit her back time to sleeping only, that will also begin to help. While it is a bit off topic, we'd also encourage as much baby-wearing as Elle can tolerate. It will help with her flat spot and, more importantly, reintegrate her in family life.

Case #3: Wilder
As you carried sweet 9-month-old Wilder to the car two weeks ago, you experienced every parent's nightmare as you slipped on a slick spot on your steps and fell. Wilder ended up with a femur fracture which is already healing well, but his abilities to do physical things this month are limited.

Wilder is going to end up with a few deficits from this experience, and that is okay. There is a lot you can do to keep him on target and even give him an edge in other areas. The other developmental milestones will come later, after his cast is off and normal life resumes.

7-9 Month Weekly Checklist

Guide	Active Baby, Healthy Brain	daily						
Visual & Verbal Skills	Reading: Indestructibles (set of 4), Day and Night: First Words Book	daily						
	Sign Language: Let's Sign, Baby!; My First Baby Signs	daily						
Motor Skills	The Amazing Peanut Ball	daily						
	Bumpie Gertie Ball	3x a week						
Social Skills	Wimmer - Ferguson Baby Mirror	daily						
Sensory Skills	Yoee Baby Fox	daily						
	Starry Night Playsilk	2x a week						
	pipSquigz Loops	2x a week						
	Taggies Crinkle Heather Hedgehog	as desired						
Developmental Play	Teethers and Tools: Bolli Teether, Amber and Wood Teething Ring, Gertie the Good Goose	as desired						
	Romeo the Greedy Toad	1-2x a week						
	Walter Squeaker	1-2x a week						

ACTIVE BABY... 7-9 MONTHS

	ACTIVITY (+ AGE IF NOTED)	MON.	TUES.	WEDS.	THURS.	FRI.
Massage	Massage					
	Massage with textures					
	Warm vs cold water					
Basic Motor Planning	Tummy time (toys, books, mirror, noises)					
	Crocodile crawling					
	Stairs					
	Obstacle courses (including under furniture)					
	Getting out of a box					
	Bobbing down for toys					
	Hold on, stand, and kick with one foot					
Upper Body	Row, Row, Row Your Boat (head lowered, hands grip)					
	Wheelbarrow					
	Rolling over a small ball					
Vestibular Stimulation	Rocking on a big ball (front, back, all ways)					
	Sitting on a roll (or peanut ball!)					
	Flying on your legs					
	Toddler swing					
	Riding or rocking on your legs					
Music & Rhythm	Hide-and-seek music					
Vision	Visual tracking					
	Posting (items go out of sight)					
	Word cards & matching					
Sensory Activities	Rolling in a blanket					
	Swinging in a blanket					
	Rolling down slopes					
	Crawling on/exploring new surfaces (prickly/soft grass, paths, sand, dirt...)					
	Pots & Pans					
	Creeping up and rolling down slopes					
	Creeping over a raised surface					
	Climbing up or creeping along a ladder					

"SEBASTIAN" SAMPLE WEEKLY CHECKLIST

Guide	Active Baby, Healthy Brain	daily					
Visual & Verbal Skills	Reading: Indestructibles (set of 4), Day and Night: First Words Book	daily					
	Sign Language: Let's Sign, Baby!; My First Baby Signs	daily					
Motor Skills	The Amazing Peanut Ball	daily					
	Bumpie Gertie Ball	3x a week					
Social Skills	Wimmer - Ferguson Baby Mirror	daily					
Sensory Skills	Yoee Baby Fox	daily					
	Starry Night Playsilk	2x a week					
	pipSquigz Loops	2x a week					
	Taggies Crinkle Heather Hedgehog	as desired					
Developmental Play	Teethers and Tools: Bolli Teether, Amber and Wood Teething Ring, Gertie the Good Goose	as desired					
	Romeo the Greedy Toad	1-2x a week					
	Walter Squeaker	1-2x a week					

Changes

This is the 9-12 month checklist, which you're pulling out to give him an appropriate challenge. Don't forget to ease into any that he finds tricky. You want to challenge and engage him - definitely not overwhelm him!

"SEBASTIAN" ACTIVE BABY... CHECKLIST

	ACTIVITY (+ AGE IF NOTED)	MON.	TUES.	WEDS.	THURS.	FRI.
Massage	Massage					
	Massage with textures					
	Warm vs cold water					
Basic Motor Planning	Tummy time (toys, books, mirror, noises)					
	Crocodile crawling					
	Stairs					
	Obstacle courses (including under furniture)					
	Getting out of a box					
	Bobbing down for toys					
	Hold on, stand, and kick with one foot					
Upper Body	Row, Row, Row Your Boat (head lowered, hands grip)					
	Wheelbarrow					
	Rolling over a small ball					
	Pull-ups (10-12 months)					
Vestibular Stimulation	Rocking on a big ball (front, back, all ways)					
	Sitting on a roll (or peanut ball!)					
	Flying on your legs					
	Toddler swing					
	Riding or rocking on your legs					
Music & Rhythm	Hide-and-seek music					
	Following simple commands (10-12 months)					
	Hold baby and dance (new holds for 10+ months)					
Vision	Visual tracking					
	Posting (items go out of sight)					
	Word cards & matching					
Sensory Activities	Rolling in a blanket					
	Swinging in a blanket					
	Crawling on/exploring new surfaces (prickly/soft grass, paths, sand, dirt...)					
	Pots & Pans					
	Creeping up and rolling down slopes					
	Creeping over a raised surface					
	Climbing up or creeping along a ladder					

2018-2019 Tiny Tots Curriculum Handbook • 800.478.0672

"ELLE" SAMPLE WEEKLY CHECKLIST

Guide	Active Baby, Healthy Brain	daily						
Visual & Verbal Skills	Reading: Indestructibles (set of 4), Day and Night: First Words Book	daily						
	Sign Language: Let's Sign, Baby!; My First Baby Signs	daily						
Motor Skills	The Amazing Peanut Ball	daily						
	Bumpie Gertie Ball	3x a week						
Social Skills	Wimmer - Ferguson Baby Mirror	daily						
Sensory Skills	Yoee Baby Fox	daily						
	Starry Night Playsilk	2x a week						
	pipSquigz Loops	2x a week						
	Taggies Crinkle Heather Hedgehog	as desired						
Developmental Play	Teethers and Tools: Bolli Teether, Amber and Wood Teething Ring, Gertie the Good Goose	as desired						
	Romeo the Greedy Toad	1-2x a week						
	Walter Squeaker	1-2x a week						

Changes
We're starting Elle with the activities for a 4-month-old. She'll likely catch up very fast, but we don't want to skip any important foundational steps.

"ELLE" ACTIVE BABY... CHECKLIST

	ACTIVITY (+ AGE IF NOTED)	MON.	TUES.	WEDS.	THURS.	FRI.
Basic Exercises	Slowly massage front & back					
	Tummy time (5 days+)					
	Leg flexing (2-3 months+)					
	Rocking sideways					
	Gentle turnovers					
	Arm movements					
	Back pushaways					
	Tummy time over a roll					
	Tummy pushaways (4 weeks+)					
	Rolling (2 months+)					
	Feet & leg reflexes (2 months+)					
	Neck & back strengthening (2 months+)					
	Rocking forward (parachute reflex)					
	Hitting/kicking a hanging balloon (2 months+)					
Upper Body	Pull-ups (3 months+)					
	Push-ups (3 months+)					
Vestibular Stimulation	Slightly inflated big ball					
	Seated rocking from side to side					
	Hammock swing					
	Stroller ride on bumpy ground					
	Stand and rock (2 months+)					
	Bobbing up & down (2 months+)					
	Rocking, rolling, bouncing on your knees (2 months+)					
	Rocking back and forth (2-3 months+)					
	Rolling on a ball (3 months+)					
	Extreme rocking on your knees (3 months+) 10x					
	"Here We Go Side to Side" (3 months+)					
Music, Rhythm, Sounds, and Song	Music & nature sounds					
	Stories, rhymes, and "conversations"					
	Dancing (head supported)					
	Bouncing and swaying on his front (4 weeks+)					
	Action rhymes (6 weeks+)					
	Tracking rattle sounds					

"WILDER" SAMPLE WEEKLY CHECKLIST

Guide	Active Baby, Healthy Brain	daily						
Visual & Verbal Skills	Reading: Indestructibles (set of 4), Day and Night: First Words Book	daily						
	Sign Language: Let's Sign, Baby!; My First Baby Signs	daily						
Motor Skills	The Amazing Peanut Ball	daily						
	Bumpie Gertie Ball	3x a week						
Social Skills	Wimmer - Ferguson Baby Mirror	daily						
Sensory Skills	Yoee Baby Fox	daily						
	Starry Night Playsilk	2x a week						
	pipSquigz Loops	2x a week						
	Taggies Crinkle Heather Hedgehog	as desired						
Developmental Play	Teethers and Tools: Bolli Teether, Amber and Wood Teething Ring, Gertie the Good Goose	as desired						
	Romeo the Greedy Toad	1-2x a week						
	Walter Squeaker	1-2x a week						

Changes

These are the standard checklists for him, but obviously you will be heavily editing many of the physical activities to suit the particulars of his cast and pain level.

"SEBASTIAN" ACTIVE BABY... CHECKLIST

	ACTIVITY (+ AGE IF NOTED)	MON.	TUES.	WEDS.	THURS.	FRI.
Massage	Massage					
	Massage with textures					
	Warm vs cold water					
Basic Motor Planning	Tummy time (toys, books, mirror, noises)					
	Crocodile crawling					
	Stairs					
	Obstacle courses (including under furniture)					
	Getting out of a box					
	Bobbing down for toys					
	Hold on, stand, and kick with one foot					
Upper Body	Row, Row, Row Your Boat (head lowered, hands grip)					
	Wheelbarrow					
	Rolling over a small ball					
Vestibular Stimulation	Rocking on a big ball (front, back, all ways)					
	Sitting on a roll (or peanut ball!)					
	Flying on your legs					
	Toddler swing					
	Riding or rocking on your legs					
Music & Rhythm	Hide-and-seek music					
Vision	Visual tracking					
	Posting (items go out of sight)					
	Word cards & matching					
Sensory Activities	Rolling in a blanket					
	Swinging in a blanket					
	Rolling down slopes					
	Crawling on/exploring new surfaces (prickly/soft grass, paths, sand, dirt...)					
	Pots & Pans					
	Creeping up and rolling down slopes					
	Creeping over a raised surface					
	Climbing up or creeping along a ladder					

10-12 Months
EAGER TO TALK AND WALK

Communication is Key
One wonderful thing about teaching your child sign language is that once he learns the principles of communication he will often shock you by simply beginning to talk instead. So know that the sign language you do now will likely pay off big time in months to come.

You'll also likely find that the more words he has (spoken or signed), the more content and happy he is. After all, if he is able to express his desires, that eliminates much of the frustration and stress in his daily life.

To help him begin to master words, encourage him to make sounds while signing. Any attempt at imitation should be cheered on, and as he progresses you'll ask for more and more precision. (That's a long way off though!) If this is his first time being exposed to signs you will want to start by modeling the signs to him and then help him copy it. For instance, sign "banana" before giving him a bite of one, then help him sign it with his hands - no precision required! Immediately, give him the banana he was "asking" for. As mentioned previously, some babies will pick up on this easily while for others it will take some time. Expect him to start getting it after a month or two - but don't be shocked if it's shorter or longer.

Set These Things Aside
Nothing! You'll be using everything in your Infant Kit these weeks.

If You Have the Tiny Tots Elite Kit (0-24 months)
Even those these items were selected for 12 months and up, your child may be ready now to get a lot of enjoyment out of these items:

Very First Book of Things to Spot set
Gertie Ball
Making Faces: A First Book of Emotions
Wee Baby Stella
ABC Baby Signs

Reading
Your baby will continue to benefit so much from the daily reading time in this season. As mentioned before, reading increases auditory processing skills, visual perception, language development, connection, and so much more. Read a book from your kit, or the library, or your bookshelf... just make sure you're reading together.

Don't Forget Sensory Input
Yoee Baby should still come out to play often. The frequent exposure helps him learn to process sensations all over his body, while also helping with bonding and so much more. The Playsilk and Bumpie Gertie Ball may be used in the same fashion, by gently rubbing/brushing/rolling on his skin. Add as many other gentle textures as you can and watch his brain grow. Bath time is also a sensory experience for him, and so is mealtime!

Case #1: Meadow, Skye, River
Yep, that's three names right there. Congratulations on your 10-month-old triplets! Your amazing little ones were delivered early and spent some time in the NICU, so 10 months is their adjusted age. Now that they are getting

mobile you will have even less one-on-one time with your babies, so what can you do to set them up for happy and healthy development?

First, relax. Yes, their life will look different from Arrow's (below), as would the life of a child added to a large family vs. a first child. They will learn from and enjoy their siblings so much in these months, and teach each other in their "down time" - talk about peer pressure!

A high priority for you is going to be implementation. What can you do to make these months' checklists easy to implement? Consider where you put the checklists (fridge? play area? changing table?), and your routine for completing items. It may be more achievable to do Peanut Ball with all three one after another rather than working River through his entire list for the day while his sisters play. You also may find a single list more efficient than managing three separate papers.

Because they have NICU history, it is likely that they have some sensory processing challenges. In that case, add "sensory" to your daily list, knowing that this could be as simple as playing on the grass in a onesie or as involved as cooking "just for play" spaghetti and letting them have a blast squashing, squeezing, and tasting it. Crawl-through tunnels are also great for sensory processing because of the visual and vestibular input they provide.

Case #2: Arrow
10-month-old Arrow is your first child, and you have the freedom to be a stay-at-home parent with no other commitments. Why not invest as much time as possible into his development?

For him, you'll be using a standard list, but also be adding in trips to the zoo, aquarium, parks, and children's museum.

You will also want to work toward letting him enjoy playing independently. Do all that you can to foster connection and enjoyment of each other, but you'll also want him to have the skill of independent exploring; working up to at least 15 minutes of solo play is appropriate for this age group. Of course, you aren't abandoning your child or isolating him - just realizing that this is yet another skill for him to learn that isn't on the list.

Case #3: Maleia
As Maleia approaches her first birthday, you notice that she doesn't use her right arm as well or as easily as she does her left. Signing is difficult, and even when she's beginning to walk you notice that her balance seems off. She's finally diagnosed with Brachial Plexus, and all the symptoms begin to make sense.

While Maleia's checklist won't change, you will want to add in any exercises that her physical therapist and occupational therapist recommend. Of course, you'll prioritize those over her routine activities to aid in her healing. The great news is that this is a very recoverable injury. You'll likely be astonished with the healing you soon see.

10-12 Month Weekly Checklist

Guide	Active Baby, Healthy Brain	daily						
Visual & Verbal Skills	Reading: Indestructibles (set of 4), Day and Night: First Words Book	daily						
	Sign Language: Let's Sign, Baby!; My First Baby Signs	daily						
Motor Skills	The Amazing Peanut Ball	daily						
	Bumpie Gertie Ball	3x a week						
Social Skills	Wimmer - Ferguson Baby Mirror	daily						
Sensory Skills	Yoee Baby Fox	daily						
	Starry Night Playsilk	2x a week						
	pipSquigz Loops	2x a week						
	Taggies Crinkle Heather Hedgehog	as desired						
Developmental Play	Teethers and Tools: Bolli Teether, Amber and Wood Teething Ring, Gertie the Good Goose	as desired						
	Romeo the Greedy Toad	1-2x a week						
	Walter Squeaker	1-2x a week						

ACTIVE BABY... 10-12 MONTHS

	ACTIVITY (+ AGE IF NOTED)	MON.	TUES.	WEDS.	THURS.	FRI.
Massage	Massage					
	Massage with textures					
	Warm vs cold water					
Basic Motor Planning	Tummy time (toys, books, mirror, noises)					
	Crocodile crawling					
	Stairs					
	Obstacle courses (including under furniture)					
	Getting out of a box					
	Bobbing down for toys					
	Hold on, stand, and kick with one foot					
Upper Body	Row, Row, Row Your Boat (head lowered, hands grip)					
	Wheelbarrow					
	Rolling over a small ball					
	Pull-ups (10-12 months)					
Vestibular Stimulation	Rocking on a big ball (front, back, all ways)					
	Sitting on a roll (or peanut ball!)					
	Flying on your legs					
	Toddler swing					
	Riding or rocking on your legs					
Music & Rhythm	Hide-and-seek music					
	Following simple commands (10-12 months)					
	Hold baby and dance (new holds for 10+ months)					
Vision	Visual tracking					
	Posting (items go out of sight)					
	Word cards & matching					
Sensory Activities	Rolling in a blanket					
	Swinging in a blanket					
	Crawling on/exploring new surfaces (prickly/soft grass, paths, sand, dirt...)					
	Pots & Pans					
	Creeping up/rolling down slopes					
	Creeping over a raised surface					
	Climbing up or creeping along a ladder					

2018-2019 Tiny Tots Curriculum Handbook • 800.478.0672

"THE TRIPLETS" WEEKLY CHECKLIST

Guide	Active Baby, Healthy Brain	daily						
Visual & Verbal Skills	Reading: Indestructibles (set of 4), Day and Night: First Words Book	daily						
	Sign Language: Let's Sign, Baby!; My First Baby Signs	daily						
Motor Skills	The Amazing Peanut Ball	daily						
	Bumpie Gertie Ball	3x a week						
Social Skills	Wimmer - Ferguson Baby Mirror	daily						
Sensory Skills	Yoee Baby Fox	daily						
	Starry Night Playsilk	2x a week						
	pipSquigz Loops	2x a week						
	Taggies Crinkle Heather Hedgehog	as desired						
Developmental Play	Teethers and Tools: Bolli Teether, Amber and Wood Teething Ring, Gertie the Good Goose	as desired						
	Romeo the Greedy Toad	1-2x a week						
	Walter Squeaker	1-2x a week						

Changes

No changes have been made, but you're going to be adjusting this list to highlight only the things your babies need to work on. For instance, if you're not going to be able to swing them in a blanket, let's take it off your list so that you are left with only achievable activities!

"THE TRIPLETS" ACTIVE BABY... CHECKLIST

	ACTIVITY (+ AGE IF NOTED)	MON.	TUES.	WEDS.	THURS.	FRI.
Massage	Massage					
	Massage with textures					
	Warm vs cold water					
Basic Motor Planning	Tummy time (toys, books, mirror, noises)					
	Crocodile crawling					
	Stairs					
	Obstacle courses (including under furniture)					
	Getting out of a box					
	Bobbing down for toys					
	Hold on, stand, and kick with one foot					
Upper Body	Row, Row, Row Your Boat (head lowered, hands grip)					
	Wheelbarrow					
	Rolling over a small ball					
	Pull-ups (10-12 months)					
Vestibular Stimulation	Rocking on a big ball (front, back, all ways)					
	Sitting on a roll (or peanut ball!)					
	Flying on your legs					
	Toddler swing					
	Riding or rocking on your legs					
Music & Rhythm	Hide-and-seek music					
	Following simple commands (10-12 months)					
	Hold baby and dance (new holds for 10+ months)					
Vision	Visual tracking					
	Posting (items go out of sight)					
	Word cards & matching					
Sensory Activities	Rolling in a blanket					
	Swinging in a blanket					
	Crawling on/exploring new surfaces (prickly/soft grass, paths, sand, dirt...)					
	Pots & Pans					
	Creeping up/rolling down slopes					
	Creeping over a raised surface					
	Climbing up or creeping along a ladder					

"ARROW" WEEKLY CHECKLIST

Guide	Active Baby, Healthy Brain	daily						
Visual & Verbal Skills	Reading: Indestructibles (set of 4), Day and Night: First Words Book	daily						
	Sign Language: Let's Sign, Baby!; My First Baby Signs	daily						
Motor Skills	The Amazing Peanut Ball	daily						
	Bumpie Gertie Ball	3x a week						
Social Skills	Wimmer - Ferguson Baby Mirror	daily						
Sensory Skills	Yoee Baby Fox	daily						
	Starry Night Playsilk	2x a week						
	pipSquigz Loops	2x a week						
	Taggies Crinkle Heather Hedgehog	as desired						
Developmental Play	Teethers and Tools: Bolli Teether, Amber and Wood Teething Ring, Gertie the Good Goose	as desired						
	Romeo the Greedy Toad	1-2x a week						
	Walter Squeaker	1-2x a week						

Changes

No changes have been made, but you're planning to add in all kinds of activities and target independent play.

"ARROW" ACTIVE BABY... CHECKLIST

	ACTIVITY (+ AGE IF NOTED)	MON.	TUES.	WEDS.	THURS.	FRI.
Massage	Massage					
	Massage with textures					
	Warm vs cold water					
Basic Motor Planning	Tummy time (toys, books, mirror, noises)					
	Crocodile crawling					
	Stairs					
	Obstacle courses (including under furniture)					
	Getting out of a box					
	Bobbing down for toys					
	Hold on, stand, and kick with one foot					
Upper Body	Row, Row, Row Your Boat (head lowered, hands grip)					
	Wheelbarrow					
	Rolling over a small ball					
	Pull-ups (10-12 months)					
Vestibular Stimulation	Rocking on a big ball (front, back, all ways)					
	Sitting on a roll (or peanut ball!)					
	Flying on your legs					
	Toddler swing					
	Riding or rocking on your legs					
Music & Rhythm	Hide-and-seek music					
	Following simple commands (10-12 months)					
	Hold baby and dance (new holds for 10+ months)					
Vision	Visual tracking					
	Posting (items go out of sight)					
	Word cards & matching					
Sensory Activities	Rolling in a blanket					
	Swinging in a blanket					
	Crawling on/exploring new surfaces (prickly/soft grass, paths, sand, dirt...)					
	Pots & Pans					
	Creeping up/rolling down slopes					
	Creeping over a raised surface					
	Climbing up or creeping along a ladder					

2018-2019 Tiny Tots Curriculum Handbook • 800.478.0672

"MALEIA" WEEKLY CHECKLIST

Guide	Active Baby, Healthy Brain	daily						
Visual & Verbal Skills	Reading: Indestructibles (set of 4), Day and Night: First Words Book	daily						
	Sign Language: Let's Sign, Baby!; My First Baby Signs	daily						
Motor Skills	The Amazing Peanut Ball	daily						
	Bumpie Gertie Ball	3x a week						
Social Skills	Wimmer - Ferguson Baby Mirror	daily						
Sensory Skills	Yoee Baby Fox	daily						
	Starry Night Playsilk	2x a week						
	pipSquigz Loops	2x a week						
	Taggies Crinkle Heather Hedgehog	as desired						
Developmental Play	Teethers and Tools: Bolli Teether, Amber and Wood Teething Ring, Gertie the Good Goose	as desired						
	Romeo the Greedy Toad	1-2x a week						
	Walter Squeaker	1-2x a week						

Changes

No changes have been made, though you are leaving room to add in any exercises from her PT/OT.

"MALEIA" ACTIVE BABY... CHECKLIST

ACTIVITY (+ AGE IF NOTED)	MON.	TUES.	WEDS.	THURS.	FRI.
Massage					
Massage					
Massage with textures					
Warm vs cold water					
Basic Motor Planning					
Tummy time (toys, books, mirror, noises)					
Crocodile crawling					
Stairs					
Obstacle courses (including under furniture)					
Getting out of a box					
Bobbing down for toys					
Hold on, stand, and kick with one foot					
Upper Body					
Row, Row, Row Your Boat (head lowered, hands grip)					
Wheelbarrow					
Rolling over a small ball					
Pull-ups (10-12 months)					
Vestibular Stimulation					
Rocking on a big ball (front, back, all ways)					
Sitting on a roll (or peanut ball!)					
Flying on your legs					
Toddler swing					
Riding or rocking on your legs					
Music & Rhythm					
Hide-and-seek music					
Following simple commands (10-12 months)					
Hold baby and dance (new holds for 10+ months)					
Vision					
Visual tracking					
Posting (items go out of sight)					
Word cards & matching					
Sensory Activities					
Rolling in a blanket					
Swinging in a blanket					
Crawling on/exploring new surfaces (prickly/soft grass, paths, sand, dirt...)					
Pots & Pans					
Creeping up/rolling down slopes					
Creeping over a raised surface					
Climbing up or creeping along a ladder					

13-16 MONTHS
LET'S GET THIS PARTY STARTED

Communication is Key
The biggest emphasis of these months will probably be in communication. Use sign language, verbal communication, or both, but let's help your child communicate! By the way, this is the single most critical thing you can do to lower his frustration/decrease tantrums and increase his connection with you.

Reading
As always, your baby will continue to benefit so much from daily reading time in this season. As mentioned before, reading increases auditory processing skills, visual perception, language development, connection, and so much more. Read a book from your kit, or the library, or your bookshelf... just make sure you're reading together.

Case #1: Emmet
At 14 months old, Emmet is hilarious and engaging. He loves to be the center of attention and learns new words daily. He is a little behind in his walking, but he now walks while holding a hand and is obviously poised to take off soon. He is not hesitant to make his desires for certain foods or toys known and has the best facial expressions.

You will definitely spend a lot of your education time working on gross motor skills with Emmet. He's ready and eager to walk, so let's do everything we can to get him there.

We'll also want to focus on speech for him, since it is an area of such strength.

Case #2: Blessing
Blessing is also 14 months old, but she's an entirely different child. She loves to walk and is quite good at it, but does not yet have any useful language. She is quite content to play for hours alone and loves taking things in and out of her play kitchen.

For Blessing, we really want to work on communication and connection. Look for opportunities to play together and have happy interactions and do everything you can to build speech (spoken or signed). We're not above food bribes at this stage. Sometimes a little extra motivation will get a child going and then you can back off the incentives as the skill becomes inherently rewarding.

Have you ever noticed that when you work with someone you grow close to them? We're going to work diligently at everything on her list - not because she lacks the physical skills but because she desperately needs to build comfortable connections. This will in turn build her desire for communication.

Case #3: Anwell

Anwell is 16 months old and very affectionate. However, you've noticed some areas of concern. For instance, if you point at a favorite toy across the room, he can't follow that point to find the toy. He seems completely confused by any pretend play and spends inordinate amounts of time lining up objects in perfect lines, or crying when some minor thing is changed in his world.

As you suspected, Anwell has many early warning signs of autism. Even as you dive into his education you will also want to work with his pediatrician for a complete assessment by an autism expert, which should unlock services for you. Hopefully you'll get access to ABA, a remarkably effective approach to helping children with autism learn.

Anwell is a child with amazing potential, but it's going to take some effort to access that. We've taken ABA courses, and have been thrilled to see its effectiveness as a tool in your toolbox. But what struck us most about that method of teaching is that it is, to oversimplify it, parenting on steroids. We were still teaching the same skills as we would otherwise, we were just breaking them down into smaller steps and doing more reps.

Anwell's checklist is heavy on speech and social skills while the rest of his chart remains standard. Adjust this to accommodate his therapy schedule, of course!

All children benefit from a clear schedule, and visual cues can also be tremendously helpful for a child who may not be able to process auditory cues in a typical fashion.

Transitions are difficult for all children, but a child with autism will struggle even more with that. Even though he has no concept of time, it can be helpful to use transitions like this:
"Anwell in 15 minutes we will be all done with the park."
"Anwell, 10 more minutes and then we need to leave the park and go get Daddy."
"Anwell, 5 minutes until we go get Daddy."
(Timer ringing) "Anwell, it's time to leave. Would you like one last trip on the slide as we leave?"

Even though it is impossible for him to know what "15 minutes" means, the rhythm and repetition will help him learn, and the ringing timer helps it feel like you're helping him cope rather than making an unfair decision about his future. You likely won't see much difference using this approach right away, but starting now will make it second-nature by the time he's two.

13–16 Months Weekly Checklist

Guide	Active Baby, Healthy Brain	daily					
Visual & Verbal Skills	Reading: Very First Books of Things to Spot set	daily					
	Sign Language: ABC Baby Signs	daily					
Motor Skills	Gertie Ball	3x a week					
	Caterpillar Stacking	1-2x a week					
	Haba Palette of Pegs	2x a week					
	Poke-A-Dot Popper	2x a week					
	Slinky Pop Toobs	2x a week					
STEM	3-D ShapeSorter	3x a week					
	Stackable Forest	1-2x a week					
	Grippies Shakers	2x a week					
Social Skills	Making Faces: A First Book of Emotions	2x a week					
	Wee Baby Stella	2x a week					
	Miffy Hide & Seek	2x a week					
Sensory Skills	Tactile Search and Match	2x a week					

ACTIVE BABY... WALKING–18 MONTHS

	ACTIVITY	MON.	TUES.	WEDS.	THURS.	FRI.
Massage	Massage					
	Massage with textures					
	Across the midline activities					
Motor Planning	Crawling on furniture					
	Walking over the rungs of a ladder					
	Creeping under furniture					
Upper Body	Row, Row, Row Your Boat					
	Monkey swing on rings					
	Throwing a ball					
Vestibular Stimulation	Balance on hills and slopes (no hands)					
	Walking backwards/sideways					
	Topsy-turvy somersault					
	Parachute reflex over a ball					
	Balance on a roll					
	Ride on a scooter board					
	Spinning					
	Beach ball stretch					
	Tipping backwards					
	Rocking on your thighs					
	Rolling down your lap					
Music & Rhythm	Rhythm activity (such as maracas or pots)					
	Dancing					
	Bobbing					
Vision	Balloon + fly swatter					
	Roll the ball back and forth					
	Parachute					
	Reading books together					
	Word & picture cards					

Note
Active Baby, Healthy Brain splits their activities at 18 months rather than at 17 months. That's why you see it go through 18 months here.

"EMMET" SAMPLE WEEKLY CHECKLIST

Category	Item	Frequency						
Guide	Active Baby, Healthy Brain	daily						
Visual & Verbal Skills	Reading: Very First Books of Things to Spot set	daily						
Visual & Verbal Skills	Sign Language: ABC Baby Signs	daily						
Motor Skills	Gertie Ball	3x a week						
Motor Skills	Caterpillar Stacking	1-2x a week						
Motor Skills	Haba Palette of Pegs	2x a week						
Motor Skills	Poke-A-Dot Popper	2x a week						
Motor Skills	Slinky Pop Toobs	2x a week						
STEM	3-D ShapeSorter	3x a week						
STEM	Stackable Forest	1-2x a week						
STEM	Grippies Shakers	2x a week						
Social Skills	Making Faces: A First Book of Emotions	2x a week						
Social Skills	Wee Baby Stella	2x a week						
Social Skills	Miffy Hide & Seek	2x a week						
Sensory Skills	Tactile Search and Match	2x a week						

Changes

Since your emphasis is on gross motor skills, try integrating that into every activity. Can he walk one step to reach that next piece? "Help" you carry the book to the favorite reading spot?

"EMMET" ACTIVE BABY... CHECKLIST

	ACTIVITY	MON.	TUES.	WEDS.	THURS.	FRI.
Massage	Massage					
	Massage with textures					
	Across the midline activities					
Motor Planning	Crawling on furniture					
	Walking over the rungs of a ladder					
	Creeping under furniture					
Upper Body	Row, Row, Row Your Boat					
	Monkey swing on rings					
	Throwing a ball					
Vestibular Stimulation	Balance on hills and slopes (no hands)					
	Walking backwards/sideways					
	Topsy-turvy somersault					
	Parachute reflex over a ball					
	Balance on a roll					
	Ride on a scooter board					
	Spinning					
	Beach ball stretch					
	Tipping backwards					
	Rocking on your thighs					
	Rolling down your lap					
Music & Rhythm	Rhythm activity (such as maracas or pots)					
	Dancing					
	Bobbing					
Vision	Balloon + fly swatter					
	Roll the ball back and forth					
	Parachute					
	Reading books together					
	Word & picture cards					

"BLESSING" SAMPLE WEEKLY CHECKLIST

Guide	Active Baby, Healthy Brain	daily					
Visual & Verbal Skills	Reading: Very First Books of Things to Spot set	daily					
	Sign Language: ABC Baby Signs	daily					
Motor Skills	Gertie Ball	3x a week					
	Caterpillar Stacking	1-2x a week					
	Haba Palette of Pegs	2x a week					
	Poke-A-Dot Popper	2x a week					
	Slinky Pop Toobs	2x a week					
STEM	3-D ShapeSorter	3x a week					
	Stackable Forest	1-2x a week					
	Grippies Shakers	2x a week					
Social Skills	Making Faces: A First Book of Emotions	daily					
	Wee Baby Stella	2x a week					
	Miffy Hide & Seek	2x a week					
Sensory Skills	Tactile Search and Match	2x a week					

Changes

As you figure out which activities Blessing enjoys, add more of those and reduce the others as needed.

"BLESSING" ACTIVE BABY... CHECKLIST

	ACTIVITY	MON.	TUES.	WEDS.	THURS.	FRI.
Massage	Massage					
	Massage with textures					
	Across the midline activities					
Motor Planning	Crawling on furniture					
	Walking over the rungs of a ladder					
	Creeping under furniture					
Upper Body	Row, Row, Row Your Boat					
	Monkey swing on rings					
	Throwing a ball					
Vestibular Stimulation	Balance on hills and slopes (no hands)					
	Walking backwards/sideways					
	Topsy-turvy somersault					
	Parachute reflex over a ball					
	Balance on a roll					
	Ride on a scooter board					
	Spinning					
	Beach ball stretch					
	Tipping backwards					
	Rocking on your thighs					
	Rolling down your lap					
Music & Rhythm	Rhythm activity (such as maracas or pots)					
	Dancing					
	Bobbing					
Vision	Balloon + fly swatter					
	Roll the ball back and forth					
	Parachute					
	Reading books together					
	Word & picture cards					

2018-2019 Tiny Tots Curriculum Handbook • 800.478.0672

"Anwell" Sample Weekly Checklist

Category	Item	Frequency						
Guide	Active Baby, Healthy Brain	daily						
Visual & Verbal Skills	Reading: Very First Books of Things to Spot set	daily						
Visual & Verbal Skills	Sign Language: ABC Baby Signs	daily						
Motor Skills	Gertie Ball	3x a week						
Motor Skills	Caterpillar Stacking	1-2x a week						
Motor Skills	Haba Palette of Pegs	2x a week						
Motor Skills	Poke-A-Dot Popper	2x a week						
Motor Skills	Slinky Pop Toobs	2x a week						
STEM	3-D ShapeSorter	3x a week						
STEM	Stackable Forest	1-2x a week						
STEM	Grippies Shakers	2x a week						
Social Skills	Making Faces: A First Book of Emotions	daily						
Social Skills	Wee Baby Stella	daily						
Social Skills	Miffy Hide & Seek	3x a week						
Sensory Skills	Tactile Search and Match	2x a week						

Changes

As Anwell begins making progress we suspect you'll find that many of these tools will be easily integrated into ABA or whatever teaching approach you're using.

"ANWELL" ACTIVE BABY… CHECKLIST

	ACTIVITY	MON.	TUES.	WEDS.	THURS.	FRI.
Massage	Massage					
	Massage with textures					
	Across the midline activities					
Motor Planning	Crawling on furniture					
	Walking over the rungs of a ladder					
	Creeping under furniture					
Upper Body	Row, Row, Row Your Boat					
	Monkey swing on rings					
	Throwing a ball					
Vestibular Stimulation	Balance on hills and slopes (no hands)					
	Walking backwards/sideways					
	Topsy-turvy somersault					
	Parachute reflex over a ball					
	Balance on a roll					
	Ride on a scooter board					
	Spinning					
	Beach ball stretch					
	Tipping backwards					
	Rocking on your thighs					
	Rolling down your lap					
Music & Rhythm	Rhythm activity (such as maracas or pots)					
	Dancing					
	Bobbing					
Vision	Balloon + fly swatter					
	Roll the ball back and forth					
	Parachute					
	Reading books together					
	Word & picture cards					

2018-2019 Tiny Tots Curriculum Handbook • 800.478.0672

17-20 Months
WE HAVE A TODDLER!

Communication is Key
The biggest emphasis of these months will probably be in communication. Use sign language, verbal communication, or both, but let's help your child communicate! This stage is so much fun, as your little one begins to let you in on what he's thinking and you are able to respond. Welcome to conversations!

Reading
As always, your baby will continue to benefit so much from daily reading time in this season. As mentioned before, reading increases auditory processing skills, visual perception, language development, connection, and so much more. Read a book from your kit, or the library, or your bookshelf... just make sure you're reading together.

Following Directions
At this age, "school work" is an invaluable training ground for obedience. You have the advantage of structure and natural opportunities to cheer your child on as he does what you've asked. You also have the ability to gently help him obey with your hand over his if he just doesn't want to this morning.

You absolutely need to be sensitive to the child who had a rough night teething, or the little one who is completely overwhelmed by the loud fireworks outside. At the same time, puzzles and other formal learning moments are the perfect opportunity to practice obeying. Fun and friendly practice will build your child's ability to persevere and we bet you'll be surprised that he will get to a point that he actually enjoys doing activities he's previously refused.

Who knows, it could even save your child's life some terrible morning when he wanders into the street and you're able to give a command and have it followed immediately.

Case #1: Hana
Charming Hana is an active, busy 18-month-old who lights up your household and has amazing fine motor skills. She loves collecting small treasures into a box or jar, then pulling them out again and again, or fitting simple puzzles together. However, she doesn't sleep well and has a lot of distress over any variance from her bedtime routine or unusual textures such as getting dirt on her hands or sitting in grass or sand. She has no words yet, and eating is challenging because there are very few foods that she will eat. She becomes very upset when any of her food spills, in fact wetness anywhere on her body (outside her diaper) is cause for many tears. You've even seen her use a washcloth to keep her breakfast milk from dripping on her - quite the sight for this petite toddler!

Hana will benefit greatly from a few interventions.

First, she sounds like a child with many sensory issues, and would likely benefit from an occupational therapy assessment/intervention plan. A good therapist will not only work on giving her the skills to handle different sensations (grass, milk, a breeze...) but will also help you learn how to help her when she is overwhelmed.

If you have the strength to wear her in a Tula or the like, that is definitely worth trying. The tight/close feeling may give her the ability to face new experiences without being overwhelmed.

It sounds like she also has a speech deficit that would benefit a ton from early intervention/speech therapy. Again, a good therapist will help you know how to help her go about building her vocabulary rather than just working with Hana and walking away. More vocabulary will go a long way toward reducing her anxiety.

Her school chart will be light on motor skills and long on language, to help her come up to speed.

Case #2: Hudson
While he is Hana's twin, handsome Hudson is in many ways Hana's opposite. He has a rapidly growing vocabulary, and loves touching all the things. He even has a good throwing arm! However Hudson sleeps a ton, spends a lot of time just sitting, and seems oblivious to all textures. He cries when put in the swing, doesn't appreciate light touches, and rages easily. His motor skills are also very lacking.

Would it shock you to learn that Hudson also has sensory processing issues? Hana's system is over-responsive while Hudson's is under responsive. Hudson also needs help processing vestibular input. If his feet are off the ground, for instance, he can't tell where he is in space and feels like you might feel if you tumbled through an avalanche and ended up head over heels with no idea which way was up. On top of that, he would be greatly benefited by targeting fine motor skills.

His chart will include an emphasis on all things fine motor. We are leaving the vestibular activities on his chart but are anticipating that we will work with his occupational therapist to determine which ones he is ready for and which ones we should set aside for a later date. The ones that we keep on the schedule after that conversation we will be heavily tailoring to him, and making them as easy as possible until he's comfortable.

17-20 Months Weekly Checklist

Category	Item	Frequency						
Guide	Active Baby, Healthy Brain	daily						
Visual & Verbal Skills	Reading: Very First Books of Things to Spot set	daily						
	Sign Language: ABC Baby Signs	daily						
Motor Skills	Gertie Ball	3x a week						
	Caterpillar Stacking	1-2x a week						
	Haba Palette of Pegs	2x a week						
	Poke-A-Dot Popper	2x a week						
	Slinky Pop Toobs	2x a week						
STEM	3-D ShapeSorter	3x a week						
	Stackable Forest	1-2x a week						
	Grippies Shakers	2x a week						
Social Skills	Making Faces: A First Book of Emotions	2x a week						
	Wee Baby Stella	2x a week						
	Miffy Hide & Seek	2x a week						
Sensory Skills	Tactile Search and Match	2x a week						

Note:

Active Baby, Healthy Brain splits their lists at 18 months, rather than 17 months. We're using the 18-24 on this page, but we wouldn't hesitate to use the 12-18 month list for a 17-month-old or any child who could use the slower pace.

ACTIVE BABY... 18-24 MONTHS

	ACTIVITY	MON.	TUES.	WEDS.	THURS.	FRI.
Motor Planning	Massage (working up to crocodile position)					
	Animal movements with starts and stops					
	Dancing with 2-3 actions					
	Moving while singing/talking					
Upper Body	Hanging from a bar or rings					
	Climbing furniture					
	Wheelbarrows					
Vestibular Stimulation	Leg hugs					
	Spinning and body parts					
	Trapeze bar					
	Wheelbarrow on ramps or beams					
	Swinging and spinning					
	Kicking with one foot					
	Steps/stairs					
	Rolling on a large ball					
	Walk on wobbly board					
Music & Rhythm	Rhythm activity such as maracas to music					
	Copy rhythm patterns					
	Rhyming movement/songs with actions					
Vision	Visual tracking with rolling games (rolling balls, ping pong balls in a hoop, in and out of tubes...)					
	Cover one eye while tracking					
	Flashlight tracking without moving head					
	Reading books/special scrapbook					
	Pretending/imitation/dress up					
Sensory Activities	Water play					
	Balloon throw & catch or beanbag hand to hand					
	Rolling balls & running to catch					
	Hitting balloons with a fly swatter					
	Standing to throw small ball					
	Hoops (sit & raise, walk around, backwards, rock in and out, step in and out, jump in)					
	Colorful ribbons (walk, heel to toe, one foot either side, sideways, jump along, tiger crawl, bear walk)					

"HANA" SAMPLE WEEKLY CHECKLIST

Category	Item	Frequency						
Guide	Active Baby, Healthy Brain	Daily						
Visual & Verbal Skills	Reading: Very First Books of Things to Spot set	daily						
	Sign Language: ABC Baby Signs	daily						
Motor Skills	Gertie Ball	3x a week						
	Caterpillar Stacking	1-2x a week						
	Haba Palette of Pegs	2x a week						
	Poke-A-Dot Popper	2x a week						
	Slinky Pop Toobs	2x a week						
STEM	3-D ShapeSorter	3x a week						
	Stackable Forest	1-2x a week						
	Grippies Shakers	2x a week						
Social Skills	Making Faces: A First Book of Emotions	daily						
	Wee Baby Stella	2x a week						
	Miffy Hide & Seek	2x a week						
Sensory Skills	Tactile Search and Match	2x a week						

Note:
We're starting Hana out with everything on a standard list, plus a slight emphasis on social skills. Of course, that anticipates that you will be using each tool to also work on language. "Can you find me the green one?" "Which one does your baby need next, diaper or bottle?" (With signs if needed) "How does he feel?" If the combination begins to feel burdensome instead of helpful, drop all the motor skills options down to once a week and really keep your focus on language.

"HANA" ACTIVE BABY... CHECKLIST

	ACTIVITY	MON.	TUES.	WEDS.	THURS.	FRI.
Motor Planning	Massage (working up to crocodile position)					
	Animal movements with starts and stops					
	Dancing with 2-3 actions					
	Moving while singing/talking					
Upper Body	Hanging from a bar or rings					
	Climbing furniture					
	Wheelbarrows					
Vestibular Stimulation	Leg hugs					
	Spinning and body parts					
	Trapeze bar					
	Wheelbarrow on ramps or beams					
	Swinging and spinning					
	Kicking with one foot					
	Steps/stairs					
	Rolling on a large ball					
	Walk on wobbly board					
Music & Rhythm	Rhythm activity such as maracas to music					
	Copy rhythm patterns					
	Rhyming movement/songs with actions					
Vision	Visual tracking with rolling games (rolling balls, ping pong balls in a hoop, in and out of tubes...)					
	Cover one eye while tracking					
	Flashlight tracking without moving head					
	Reading books/special scrapbook					
	Pretending/imitation/dress up					
Sensory Activities	Water play					
	Balloon throw & catch or beanbag hand to hand					
	Rolling balls & running to catch					
	Hitting balloons with a fly swatter					
	Standing to throw small ball					
	Hoops (sit & raise, walk around, backwards, rock in and out, step in and out, jump in)					
	Colorful ribbons (walk, heel to toe, one foot either side, sideways, jump along, tiger crawl, bear walk)					

"HUDSON" SAMPLE WEEKLY CHECKLIST

Guide	Active Baby, Healthy Brain	daily					
Visual & Verbal Skills	Reading: Very First Books of Things to Spot set	daily					
	Sign Language: ABC Baby Signs	daily					
Motor Skills	Gertie Ball	daily					
	Caterpillar Stacking	daily					
	Haba Palette of Pegs	daily					
	Poke-A-Dot Popper	daily					
	Slinky Pop Toobs	daily					
STEM	3-D ShapeSorter	daily					
	Stackable Forest	daily					
	Grippies Shakers	daily					
Social Skills	Making Faces: A First Book of Emotions	2x a week					
	Wee Baby Stella	2x a week					
	Miffy Hide & Seek	2x a week					
Sensory Skills	Tactile Search and Match	2x a week					

Note:

Hudson has a ton of "daily" activities on this list. Don't feel overwhelmed by that, but just work in as many as you can. It may become natural to do one or two after each meal/snack. Or perhaps you could set a timer for an hour, do one tool, then reset it for another hour and repeat. Find a strategy that works for you - or completely ignore the list if he's become excited to drop raisins down a paper towel tube. After all, why pull him off the fine motor activity he chose in order to do one that may not captivate him quite as readily at this very moment?

"HUDSON" ACTIVE BABY... CHECKLIST

	ACTIVITY	MON.	TUES.	WEDS.	THURS.	FRI.
Motor Planning	Massage (working up to crocodile position)					
	Animal movements with starts and stops					
	Dancing with 2-3 actions					
	Moving while singing/talking					
Upper Body	Hanging from a bar or rings					
	Climbing furniture					
	Wheelbarrows					
Vestibular Stimulation	Leg hugs					
	Spinning and body parts					
	Trapeze bar					
	Wheelbarrow on ramps or beams					
	Swinging and spinning					
	Kicking with one foot					
	Steps/stairs					
	Rolling on a large ball					
	Walk on wobbly board					
Music & Rhythm	Rhythm activity such as maracas to music					
	Copy rhythm patterns					
	Rhyming movement/songs with actions					
Vision	Visual tracking with rolling games (rolling balls, ping pong balls in a hoop, in and out of tubes...)					
	Cover one eye while tracking					
	Flashlight tracking without moving head					
	Reading books/special scrapbook					
	Pretending/imitation/dress up					
Sensory Activities	Water play					
	Balloon throw & catch or beanbag hand to hand					
	Rolling balls & running to catch					
	Hitting balloons with a fly swatter					
	Standing to throw small ball					
	Hoops (sit & raise, walk around, backwards, rock in and out, step in and out, jump in)					
	Colorful ribbons (walk, heel to toe, one foot either side, sideways, jump along, tiger crawl, bear walk)					

21-24 Months
A FUNNY AND OPINIONATED LITTLE PERSON!

Mastering Communication
The biggest emphasis of these months will continue to be communication. Use sign language, verbal communication, or both, but let's help your child communicate! As an added benefit, as your child gains words, you gain insight into his amazing and funny personality. This age is beyond phenomenal and you're going to love hearing what's going through his head!

Side note: You're going to hear a lot of "NO!" around your house. Your child loves being able to make his own choices now and won't hesitate to make his opinion known. To minimize stress, really work at only asking him if you are ready for his answer. Don't ask, "Can I buckle you up before we leave?" if you must leave this minute and will be buckling him regardless of his answer. It would be better to tell him, "I need to buckle you up now, would you like to hold the car or the doll while we're driving?" That lets him have control over what he can have control over, and leaves you asking when you're asking and telling/directing when the choice is strictly yours.

Reading
As always, your toddler will continue to benefit so much from daily reading time. As mentioned before, reading increases auditory processing skills, visual perception, language development, connection, and so much more. Read a book from your kit or the library or your bookshelf... just make sure you're reading together.

Case #1: Ember
If you look up firecracker in the dictionary, you'll probably find a picture of Ember. She loves to push, pull, run, dance... anything physical. She spins endlessly, runs full steam ahead into things, and climbs and jumps off of everything. She chews on anything she can get her hands on, is a huge fan of loud noises, and touches everything.

Busy Ember has another type of sensory processing disorder, known as sensory seeking. She needs aggressive physical input to calm and regulate her body, and to help her know where she is in space. As you likely suspect, we'd highly recommend an assessment with an occupational therapist and integration of the OT's plan in everyday life.

Getting her to sit down for any of the STEM skills may be tough. You could try setting the pieces across the room and have her run and grab one, then run back, slamming into a giant beanbag before placing the piece. That may regulate her brain enough to be able to think. Try moving quiet activities, like reading, to immediately after challenging physical activities, such as Active Baby... or Gertie Ball.

Ember may be your most challenging student this year, but the rewards will pay off as you help her bring her body into balance and use some of her untapped energy.

Case #2: Owen
When Owen was born, you were shocked to learn that he has Down Syndrome. 2 years later, you are so in love with him that you rarely consider that. However, there are some delays that Owen works with every day. His low muscle tone has made it hard for him to walk or talk. His motor skills are at about the level of a 14-month-old, as are his verbal skills.

However, his comprehension is at age level and he loves all things that move.

For Owen, you're going to want to move back to the most appropriate activities for him, which will be the 13-16 month list. You'll also want to really emphasize sign language for him, to give him the communication he so desperately needs. As he continues to grow and develop, it's going to be most helpful if you just walk through the tools at whatever pace he needs. You may find he hit growth spurts and suddenly is ready for activities for a 20-month-old, or, even more likely, that he is ready for age-appropriate skills in Social/Emotional, but lags a bit in motor skills. Who cares? Just let him enjoy life at his pace, and be ready to provide the next level for him when he gets there. Because chances are, he'll be there soon!

Case #3: Sage
Since birth Sage has been a very visual learner, and it didn't take long for her to become a great little conversationalist as well. She shares your love for books, and seemed extraordinarily interested in learning to read. Being an advocate for early education, you made her sight word flashcards, which she loves. She really read for the first time at 16 months, and now at 22 months still absolutely loves to read. Most people are skeptical of her skills until they actually see her in action.

First off, this is amazing! How impressive that you cultivated her interest and developed a very real skill so early!

Secondly, you are going to want to make sure that you continue to fuel her delight, instead of quenching the flame. Take the time to ask yourself if the activities you select are in any way crushing her spirit, but don't let that fear keep you from capitalizing on the strength God has given this little one.

For her chart, we're going to add in All About Reading. Yes, it's unheard of. Yes, you're going to take flack for this at the next homeschool group meeting. However, it is what Sage is ready for, and of all the experts in the world, you're hers! Do the placement test with her, then put her at the appropriate level. Of course, she won't be able to do the fine motor portions of the work, but she's going to love the reading.

We'll keep the rest of her chart standard. We don't want her to abandon all other skills while she chases this one - but we do want to encourage her in her gifting.

P.S. This is the actual story of one of the original Timberdoodle Kids. And yes, she still loves reading!

Weekly Checklist (Toddler Kit)

Category	Item	Frequency					
Guide	Active Baby, Healthy Brain	daily					
Visual & Verbal Skills	Reading: Very First Books of Things to Spot set	daily					
Visual & Verbal Skills	Sign Language: ABC Baby Signs	daily					
Motor Skills	Gertie Ball	3x a week					
Motor Skills	Caterpillar Stacking	1-2x a week					
Motor Skills	Haba Palette of Pegs	2x a week					
Motor Skills	Poke-A-Dot Popper	2x a week					
Motor Skills	Slinky Pop Toobs	2x a week					
STEM	3-D ShapeSorter	3x a week					
STEM	Stackable Forest	1-2x a week					
STEM	Grippies Shakers	2x a week					
Social Skills	Making Faces: A First Book of Emotions	2x a week					
Social Skills	Wee Baby Stella	2x a week					
Social Skills	Miffy Hide & Seek	2x a week					
Sensory Skills	Tactile Search and Match	2x a week					

ACTIVE BABY... 18-24 MONTHS

	ACTIVITY	MON.	TUES.	WEDS.	THURS.	FRI.
Motor Planning	Massage (working up to crocodile position)					
	Animal movements with starts and stops					
	Dancing with 2-3 actions					
	Moving while singing/talking					
Upper Body	Hanging from a bar or rings					
	Climbing furniture					
	Wheelbarrows					
Vestibular Stimulation	Leg hugs					
	Spinning and body parts					
	Trapeze bar					
	Wheelbarrow on ramps or beams					
	Swinging and spinning					
	Kicking with one foot					
	Steps/stairs					
	Rolling on a large ball					
	Walk on wobbly board					
Music & Rhythm	Rhythm activity such as maracas to music					
	Copy rhythm patterns					
	Rhyming movement/songs with actions					
Vision	Visual tracking with rolling games (rolling balls, ping pong balls in a hoop, in and out of tubes…)					
	Cover one eye while tracking					
	Flashlight tracking without moving head					
	Reading books/special scrapbook					
	Pretending/imitation/dress up					
Sensory Activities	Water play					
	Balloon throw & catch or beanbag hand to hand					
	Rolling balls & running to catch					
	Hitting balloons with a fly swatter					
	Standing to throw small ball					
	Hoops (sit & raise, walk around, backwards, rock in and out, step in and out, jump in)					
	Colorful ribbons (walk, heel to toe, one foot either side, sideways, jump along, tiger crawl, bear walk)					

"EMBER" SAMPLE CHECKLIST

Category	Item	Frequency					
Guide	Active Baby, Healthy Brain	daily					
Visual & Verbal Skills	Reading: Very First Books of Things to Spot set	daily					
	Sign Language: ABC Baby Signs	daily					
Motor Skills	Gertie Ball	3x a week					
	Caterpillar Stacking	1-2x a week					
	Haba Palette of Pegs	2x a week					
	Poke-A-Dot Popper	2x a week					
	Slinky Pop Toobs	2x a week					
STEM	3-D ShapeSorter	3x a week					
	Stackable Forest	1-2x a week					
	Grippies Shakers	2x a week					
Social Skills	Making Faces: A First Book of Emotions	2x a week					
	Wee Baby Stella	2x a week					
	Miffy Hide & Seek	2x a week					
Sensory Skills	Tactile Search and Match	2x a week					

Note:

You're going to start with a standard list for Ember and then tailor it as you go. If it works well for her to integrate large muscle input with the STEM and motor skills, run with it, literally. If that's challenging, then back off whatever you need to in order to keep her productive and keep completing OT goals.

"EMBER" ACTIVE BABY... CHECKLIST

	ACTIVITY	MON.	TUES.	WEDS.	THURS.	FRI.
	Massage (working up to crocodile position)					
Motor Planning	Animal movements with starts and stops					
	Dancing with 2-3 actions					
	Moving while singing/talking					
Upper Body	Hanging from a bar or rings					
	Climbing furniture					
	Wheelbarrows					
Vestibular Stimulation	Leg hugs					
	Spinning and body parts					
	Trapeze bar					
	Wheelbarrow on ramps or beams					
	Swinging and spinning					
	Kicking with one foot					
	Steps/stairs					
	Rolling on a large ball					
	Walk on wobbly board					
Music & Rhythm	Rhythm activity such as maracas to music					
	Copy rhythm patterns					
	Rhyming movement/songs with actions					
Vision	Visual tracking with rolling games (rolling balls, ping pong balls in a hoop, in and out of tubes...)					
	Cover one eye while tracking					
	Flashlight tracking without moving head					
	Reading books/special scrapbook					
	Pretending/imitation/dress up					
Sensory Activities	Water play					
	Balloon throw & catch or beanbag hand to hand					
	Rolling balls & running to catch					
	Hitting balloons with a fly swatter					
	Standing to throw small ball					
	Hoops (sit & raise, walk around, backwards, rock in and out, step in and out, jump in)					
	Colorful ribbons (walk, heel to toe, one foot either side, sideways, jump along, tiger crawl, bear walk)					

"OWEN" SAMPLE CHECKLIST

Guide	Active Baby, Healthy Brain	daily					
Visual & Verbal Skills	Reading: Very First Books of Things to Spot set	daily					
	Sign Language: ABC Baby Signs	daily					
Motor Skills	Gertie Ball	3x a week					
	Caterpillar Stacking	1-2x a week					
	Haba Palette of Pegs	2x a week					
	Poke-A-Dot Popper	2x a week					
	Slinky Pop Toobs	2x a week					
STEM	3-D ShapeSorter	3x a week					
	Stackable Forest	1-2x a week					
	Grippies Shakers	2x a week					
Social Skills	Making Faces: A First Book of Emotions	2x a week					
	Wee Baby Stella	2x a week					
	Miffy Hide & Seek	2x a week					
Sensory Skills	Tactile Search and Match	2x a week					

Note:

You'll find that this side of the page has the same tools as Owen's peers. The only difference is in your expectations. Just like with a "typical" 14-month-old, you'll be doing a lot of scaffolding and assisting as he gets the hang of each of these.

"OWEN" ACTIVE BABY... CHECKLIST

	ACTIVITY	MON.	TUES.	WEDS.	THURS.	FRI.
Massage	Massage					
	Massage with textures					
	Across the midline activities					
Motor Planning	Crawling on furniture					
	Walking over the rungs of a ladder					
	Creeping under furniture					
Upper Body	Row, Row, Row Your Boat					
	Monkey swing on rings					
	Throwing a ball					
Vestibular Stimulation	Balance on hills and slopes (no hands)					
	Walking backwards/sideways					
	Topsy-turvy somersault					
	Parachute reflex over a ball					
	Balance on a roll					
	Ride on a scooter board					
	Spinning					
	Beach ball stretch					
	Tipping backwards					
	Rocking on your thighs					
	Rolling down your lap					
Music & Rhythm	Rhythm activity (such as maracas or pots)					
	Dancing					
	Bobbing					
Vision	Balloon + fly swatter					
	Roll the ball back and forth					
	Parachute					
	Reading books together					
	Word & picture cards					

2018-2019 Tiny Tots Curriculum Handbook • 800.478.0672

"SAGE" SAMPLE CHECKLIST

Category	Item	Frequency					
Guide	Active Baby, Healthy Brain	Daily					
Visual & Verbal Skills	Reading: Very First Books of Things to Spot set, ABC Baby Signs	daily					
	All About Reading	daily					
Motor Skills	Gertie Ball	3x a week					
	Caterpillar Stacking	1-2x a week					
	Haba Palette of Pegs	2x a week					
	Poke-A-Dot Popper	2x a week					
	Slinky Pop Toobs	2x a week					
STEM	3-D ShapeSorter	3x a week					
	Stackable Forest	1-2x a week					
	Grippies Shakers	2x a week					
Social Skills	Making Faces: A First Book of Emotions	2x a week					
	Wee Baby Stella	2x a week					
	Miffy Hide & Seek	2x a week					
Sensory Skills	Tactile Search and Match	2x a week					

Note:

The big difference on Sage's list is simply the addition of All About Reading. Go at her pace, of course, but don't hesitate to go as fast and far as she's eager to go. The rest of her list is standard to help you make sure that she doesn't fall behind in any other areas. You may find that her knack for reading makes teaching social skills with library books more effective than simply using the one book that's included. If so, supplement away!

"SAGE" ACTIVE BABY... CHECKLIST

	ACTIVITY	MON.	TUES.	WEDS.	THURS.	FRI.
Motor Planning	Massage (working up to crocodile position)					
	Animal movements with starts and stops					
	Dancing with 2-3 actions					
	Moving while singing/talking					
Upper Body	Hanging from a bar or rings					
	Climbing furniture					
	Wheelbarrows					
Vestibular Stimulation	Leg hugs					
	Spinning and body parts					
	Trapeze bar					
	Wheelbarrow on ramps or beams					
	Swinging and spinning					
	Kicking with one foot					
	Steps/stairs					
	Rolling on a large ball					
	Walk on wobbly board					
Music & Rhythm	Rhythm activity such as maracas to music					
	Copy rhythm patterns					
	Rhyming movement/songs with actions					
Vision	Visual tracking with rolling games (rolling balls, ping pong balls in a hoop, in and out of tubes...)					
	Cover one eye while tracking					
	Flashlight tracking without moving head					
	Reading books/special scrapbook					
	Pretending/imitation/dress up					
Sensory Activities	Water play					
	Balloon throw & catch or beanbag hand to hand					
	Rolling balls & running to catch					
	Hitting balloons with a fly swatter					
	Standing to throw small ball					
	Hoops (sit & raise, walk around, backwards, rock in and out, step in and out, jump in)					
	Colorful ribbons (walk, heel to toe, one foot either side, sideways, jump along, tiger crawl, bear walk)					

2018-2019 Tiny Tots Curriculum Handbook • 800.478.0672

READING CHALLENGE
BASED ON THE READING CHALLENGE FOR KIDS FROM REDEEMEDREADER.COM

The Reading Challenge for Kids will get you and your tiny one reading a broader variety of books this year and perhaps discovering new favorites. This reading challenge is used with permission from the fine folks at RedeemedReader.com. Check out their website for more information about this reading challenge, and for great book reviews and book suggestions for your kids.

When You Are the Reader
For your little baby or toddler, you'll be looking for simple picture and board books that fit the guidelines. This can be both fun and challenging, as many categories can be filled easily or with a little creativity. But if you hit a category that stumps you, don't sweat it, just skip to the next one. Or if you'd like to hit the full number of books this year, simply substitute a household favorite for each tough category.

How It Works
On the following pages, you'll find four lists of books which you are meant to read one after another this year. Not all families will make it through all the lists, so you will need to choose a reading goal early in the year and set your pace accordingly.

Goal #1: The Light Reader
This plan has 13 books, which sets a pace of one book every four weeks.

Goal #2: The Avid Reader
The Avid Reader plan adds another 13 books, which increases the pace to one book every two weeks.

Goal #3: The Committed Reader
This plan adds a further 26 books, bringing the total to 52, or 1 book every week.

Goal #4: The Obsessed Reader
The Obsessed Reader plan doubles the total yet again, bringing it to 104 books, which sets a pace of 2 books every week.

Getting Started
Begin with the Light plan, which includes suggestions for 13 books. Choose those books and read them in any order, checking them off as you complete them. Next, advance to the Avid plan, using the criteria there to choose another 13 books and read them in any order. Then it's time to move to the Committed plan with a further 26 books, again reading them in any order. If you have completed the Committed plan (that's 52 books so far!), you are ready to brave the Obsessed plan. If you want to finish your books in a school year or before a milestone (such as a second birthday) rather than in an entire calendar year, the timeline shifts a bit, so be sure to set your goal at the beginning of the year and pace yourself accordingly.

Will This Be Expensive?
It doesn't need to be. You can read library books and e-versions, buy used, borrow from friends, and scour your family bookshelves.

Customize the Plan
Here are three ideas to incorporate reading into your family's busy schedule and unique schooling style:

1. Incorporate a reading time into your existing bedtime routine, family devotions, car time, snack time, or other routine.

2. Have an older sibling read to your little one as part of their school lessons. The older sibling will gain fluency as your little one soaks up the one-on-one time.

3. Plan some overlap between your baby's booklist and that of an older child. Not only will this accomplish two children's reading goals at once, it will also be a great "together" activity.

Let's Read!
Pick your plan, choose some books with your child, and get started! Here's the pace for a 36-week schedule:

Light Reader: One book every two to three weeks.

Avid Reader: One book every week or two.

Committed Reader: One and a half books every week.

Obsessed Reader: Almost three books every week.

THE LIGHT READER

The Challenge	The Book You Chose	Date Completed
1. A book about something true		
2. A biography		
3. A classic novel/story		
4. A book your grandparent (or other relative) says was his/her favorite at your age		
5. An old true story		
6. A book about something you love		
7. A book made into a movie (but read the book first!)		
8. A book that someone at least twice your age recommends		
9. A book more than 100 years old		
10. A picture book		
11. A mystery or detective novel		
12. A book published in 2018-2109		
13. A book about a current issue		

THE AVID READER

The Challenge	The Book You Chose	Date Completed
14. A book of fairy tales (or an extended retelling of one)		
15. A book recommended by a parent or sibling		
16. A book by or about an international traveler		
17. A Caldecott, Newbery, or Geisel Award winner		
18. A book about a holiday		
19. A book at least ten times the length of your age (e.g., if you are eight, then read a book at least 80 pages long)		
20. A book by an author you recently heard quoted		
21. A book that has a fruit in its title		
22. A book with a great cover		
23. A book that ties into pop culture (e.g., something about Star Wars)		
24. A book about your region's history		
25. A graphic novel		
26. A book of poetry		

THE COMMITTED READER

The Challenge	The Book You Chose	Date Completed
27. A book about a religion (or someone who professes a religion)		
28. A book written by an author with an initial in his or her name (e.g., C.S. Lewis)		
29. A book that won an award in 2017 or 2018		
30. A book about an adventure		
31. A play by William Shakespeare (or a retelling of one of his plays)		
32. A funny book		
33. A book based on a true story		
34. An easy reader classic (e.g., A Bargain for Frances, Frog and Toad, Little Bear, etc.)		
35. A book by or about a famous American		
36. A wordless book		
37. A book with a one-word title		
38. A book about money, finance, or earning money		
39. A story set in a different country		

THE COMMITTED READER, CONT.

The Challenge	The Book You Chose	Date Completed
40. A book about music or a musician		
41. A book about an invention or inventor		
42. A book about joy or happiness		
43. A book about a boy		
44. A book with a title that comes from another book (a famous quote, verse, etc.)		
45. A book you have started but never finished		
46. A book about a skill you want to learn		
47. A book about someone who is differently abled (blind, deaf, mentally handicapped, etc.)		
48. A book you or your family owns but you've never read		
49. A book about babies		
50. A book about a girl		
51. A book featuring someone of a different ethnicity than you		
52. A book written by someone of a different ethnicity than you		

THE OBSESSED READER

The Challenge	The Book You Chose	Date Completed
53. A book recommended by a librarian or teacher		
54. An alphabet book		
55. A book by a first-time author		
56. A biography of a world leader		
57. A book published the same year you were born		
58. A book about food		
59. A book about service		
60. A book about relationships or friendship		
61. A book about siblings		
62. A book about animals		
63. A book about art or artists		
64. A book with sparkles		
65. A book about communication		
66. A book about families		
67. A book about a hobby		
68. A book of comics		
69. A book about a famous war		
70. A book about sports		
71. A book about math (numbers, mathematicians, patterns, ...)		
72. A book about suffering or poverty		
73. A book by your favorite author		
74. A book you've read before		
75. If you're a girl: a book about being a girl; if you're a boy: a book about being a boy		
76. A book about someone else's favorite subject (perhaps your brother loves trucks or your grandma loves flowers?)		
77. A book highlighting someone your age		
78. A book about the natural world		

THE OBSESSED READER, CONT.

The Challenge	The Book You Chose	Date Completed
79. A biography of an author		
80. A nonfiction book about something historical		
81. A historical fiction book		
82. A book about science or a scientist		
83. A book about a country or city		
84. A book about space or an astronaut		
85. A book with an ugly cover		
86. A book about a martyr		
87. A book about writing		
88. A book about ancient history		
89. A book about medieval history		
90. A book from the 0-100 Dewey Decimal section of your library		
91. A book from Dewey Decimal 100-200		
92. A book from Dewey Decimal 200-300		
93. A book from Dewey Decimal 300-400 (look for the fairy tales and fables in the 398.2 section)		
94. A book from Dewey Decimal 400-500		
95. A book from Dewey Decimal 500-600		
96. A book from Dewey Decimal 600-700		
97. A book from Dewey Decimal 700-800		
98. A book from Dewey Decimal 800-900 (look for the 811 section for poetry!)		
99. A book from Dewey Decimal 900-1000		
100. A book about making friends		
101. A book about sickness/emergencies		
102. A book about adoption		
103. A photo essay book		
104. A book written in the 20th century		

LEARNING TOGETHER

THERE'S SO MUCH TO LEARN!

Once your baby is safely home, you will want to do more with him than "just" feed him and keep him warm. You'll want to begin to interact and build a relationship. However, you'll also want to make this easy to implement since you're running on what is likely the least sleep of your life.

This book will do the trick. It is packed with information and ideas to help you get to know your little one better, while also showing you how to help him grow and develop in a balanced manner, making the most of his amazing brain. You're going to have a blast!

ACTIVE BABY, HEALTHY BRAIN

INFANT ~ TODDLER ~ TINY TOTS ELITE

Babies crave more than a meal and a cuddle. They are eager, voracious learners. Many new parents are just as enthusiastic to start homeschooling their babies, but they don't know where to start.

Active Baby, Healthy Brain is the most practical handbook for all parents enthralled with every aspect of their baby's intellectual and physical development. It is simple and to the point, with ideas that are quick and easy to implement. Each activity is presented with detailed, step-by-step instructions, and the appealing illustrations help to make everything crystal clear.

And while the overall tone is one of having fun with your baby—and you will—the author makes sure you understand the crucial connections between the activities and the development of your baby's body and brain.

Busy parents cheer! No single activity takes more than 2 minutes, and all that's required is 10 minutes a day. Yet when we tried to implement the daily instructions with our foster babies, we found it hard to remember what exactly we were supposed to do each day.

The lists on pages 94-97 of this handbook are not designed to replace the book in any way. (Our notes are cryptic at best, and you will definitely need the often-illustrated instructions in the book itself.) But after familiarizing yourself with this season's activities, just use these checklists to make sure you're not forgetting any activities this week.

Caution
It is vital that you never allow your baby's head to flop–always support the head and neck and modify or skip the activity if your baby is not yet strong enough. For those of you with preemies or babies with other special needs, do take into account adjusted age and current ability. This program is designed to be ability-based and not age-dictated, so work through it at your child's pace.

Scheduling
Unless otherwise noted, you'll want to do each activity one to three times a day at most. (The one exception is massage–work that into your baby's day just as often as you can. The sensory integration is priceless!) Since most activities take 30 seconds or less, this is definitely not as time-intensive as you might think at first glance!

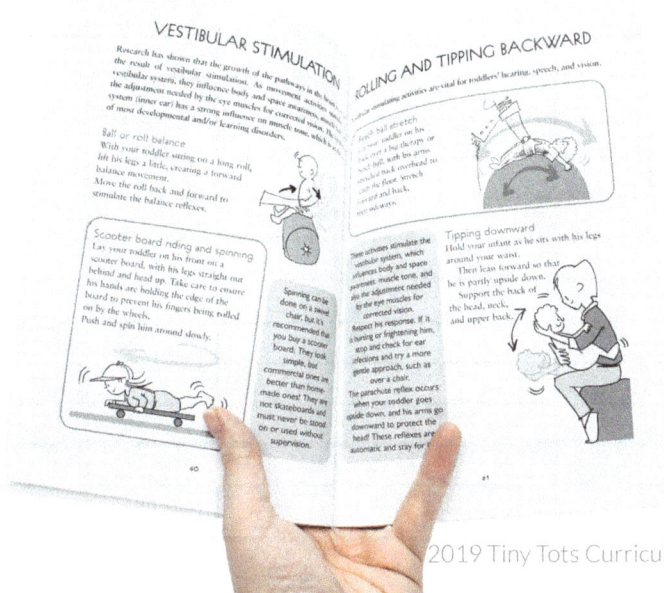

ACTIVE BABY... 0-6 MONTHS

	ACTIVITY	MON.	TUES.	WEDS.	THURS.	FRI.
Basic Exercises	Slowly massage front & back					
	Tummy time (5 days+)					
	Leg flexing (2-3 months+)					
	Rocking sideways					
	Gentle turnovers					
	Arm movements					
	Back pushaways					
	Tummy time over a roll					
	Tummy pushaways (4 weeks+)					
	Rolling (2 months+)					
	Feet & leg reflexes (2 months+)					
	Neck & back strengthening (2 months+)					
	Rocking forward (parachute reflex)					
	Hitting/kicking a hanging balloon (2 months+)					
Upper Body	Pull-ups (3 months+)					
	Push-ups (3 months+)					
Vestibular Stimulation	Slightly inflated big ball					
	Seated rocking from side to side					
	Hammock swing					
	Stroller ride on bumpy ground					
	Stand and rock (2 months+)					
	Bobbing up & down (2 months+)					
	Rocking, rolling, bouncing on your knees (2 months+)					
	Rocking back and forth (2-3 months+)					
	Rolling on a ball (3 months+)					
	Extreme rocking on your knees (3 months+) 10x					
	"Here We Go Side to Side" (3 months+)					
Music, Rhythm, and Song	Music & nature sounds					
	Stories, rhymes, and "conversations"					
	Dancing (head supported)					
	Bouncing and swaying on his front (4 weeks+)					
	Action rhymes (6 weeks+)					
Vision	Flickering lights (0-2 months) 4x/day					
	Tracking rattle sounds					

www.timberdoodle.com • ©2018

ACTIVE BABY... 6-12 MONTHS

	ACTIVITY	MON.	TUES.	WEDS.	THURS.	FRI.
Massage	Massage					
	Massage with textures					
	Warm vs cold water					
Basic Motor Planning	Tummy time (toys, books, mirror, noises)					
	Crocodile crawling					
	Stairs					
	Obstacle courses (including under furniture)					
	Getting out of a box					
	Bobbing down for toys					
	Hold on, stand, and kick with one foot					
Upper Body	Row, Row, Row Your Boat (head lowered, hands grip)					
	Wheelbarrow					
	Rolling over a small ball					
	Pull-ups (10-12 months)					
Vestibular Stimulation	Rocking on a big ball (front, back, all ways)					
	Sitting on a roll (or peanut ball!)					
	Flying on your legs					
	Toddler swing					
	Riding or rocking on your legs					
Music & Rhythm	Hide-and-seek music					
	Following simple commands (10-12 months)					
	Hold baby and dance (new holds for 10+ months)					
Vision	Visual tracking					
	Posting (items go out of sight)					
	Word cards & matching					
Sensory Activities	Rolling in a blanket					
	Swinging in a blanket					
	Rolling down slopes					
	Crawling on/exploring new surfaces (prickly/soft grass, paths, sand, dirt...)					
	Pots & Pans					
	Creeping up and rolling down slopes					
	Creeping over a raised surface					
	Climbing up or creeping along a ladder					

ACTIVE BABY... WALKING—18 MONTHS

	ACTIVITY	MON.	TUES.	WEDS.	THURS.	FRI.
Massage	Massage					
	Massage with textures					
	Across the midline activities					
Motor Planning	Crawling on furniture					
	Walking over the rungs of a ladder					
	Creeping under furniture					
Upper Body	Row, Row, Row Your Boat					
	Monkey swing on rings					
	Throwing a ball					
Vestibular Stimulation	Balance on hills and slopes (no hands)					
	Walking backwards/sideways					
	Topsy-turvy somersault					
	Parachute reflex over a ball					
	Balance on a roll					
	Ride on a scooter board					
	Spinning					
	Beach ball stretch					
	Tipping backwards					
	Rocking on your thighs					
	Rolling down your lap					
Music & Rhythm	Rhythm activity (such as maracas or pots)					
	Dancing					
	Bobbing					
Vision	Balloon + fly swatter					
	Roll the ball back and forth					
	Parachute					
	Reading books together					
	Word & picture cards					

ACTIVE BABY... 18-24 MONTHS

	ACTIVITY	MON.	TUES.	WEDS.	THURS.	FRI.
Motor Planning	Massage (working up to crocodile position)					
	Animal movements with starts and stops					
	Dancing with 2-3 actions					
	Moving while singing/talking					
Upper Body	Hanging from a bar or rings					
	Climbing furniture					
	Wheelbarrows					
Vestibular Stimulation	Leg hugs					
	Spinning and body parts					
	Trapeze bar					
	Wheelbarrow on ramps or beams					
	Swinging and spinning					
	Kicking with one foot					
	Steps/stairs					
	Rolling on a large ball					
	Walk on wobbly board					
Music & Rhythm	Rhythm activity such as maracas to music					
	Copy rhythm patterns					
	Rhyming movement/songs with actions					
Vision	Visual tracking with rolling games (rolling balls, ping pong balls in a hoop, in and out of tubes...)					
	Cover one eye while tracking					
	Flashlight tracking without moving head					
	Reading books/special scrapbook					
	Pretending/imitation/dress up					
Sensory Activities	Water play					
	Balloon throw & catch or beanbag hand to hand					
	Rolling balls & running to catch					
	Hitting balloons with a fly swatter					
	Standing to throw small ball					
	Hoops (sit & raise, walk around, backwards, rock in and out, step in and out, jump in)					
	Colorful ribbons (walk, heel to toe, one foot either side, sideways, jump along, tiger crawl, bear walk)					

2018-2019 Tiny Tots Curriculum Handbook • 800.478.0672

VISUAL AND VERBAL SKILLS

THREE TIPS ON LANGUAGE DEVELOPMENT

Stop for a moment and marvel at the comprehension needed for your little one to follow simple directions, ask for a favorite snack, or even express her delight in seeing her mother.

The number one thing you can do for language development is to simply talk with your child. You'll be astonished at how much of your vocabulary she can quote by age two!

The second is just as achievable – read together. Reading develops vocabulary in great part because it provides a structured way to talk with your child about things you may not otherwise discuss.

Third, sign language is a truly remarkable tool—use it! Your child will be able to talk to you long before she figures out how to make her mouth work as she wants.

What's the bottom line? It's the same tool with three different techniques. Talk; it's going to make all the difference!

INDESTRUCTIBLES

INFANT ~ ~~TODDLER~~ ~ TINY TOTS ELITE

Parents of infants have enough to worry about without trying to safeguard their baby's reading material. Chew-proof, rip-proof, and non-toxic, Indestructibles are built for the way babies read!

Made of incredible paper-like material for your baby to hold, grab, chew, pull, and bend, Indestructibles can handle it all. Bright and swirling with color, these wordless books allow parents' stories to be as rich as the artwork.

And for those inevitable encounters with food or its by-products, parents will be relieved to know they can just toss an Indestructible book into the wash.

Scheduling
Give your little one free access to these books while teething. As he gets older, use the illustrations of these wordless books to inspire your creative, impromptu stories.

Day and Night First Words

INFANT ~ ~~TODDLER~~ ~ TINY TOTS ELITE

Most babies don't like tummy time, not only because it can be uncomfortable after a meal, but also because it takes so much work to enjoy their surroundings. Yet babies are not only occupying large amounts of time on their backs but also spending time in car seats, bouncy seats, and front carriers that restrict them from turning their heads from side to side to give them lovely rounded heads. So babies need to spend more waking hours on their tummies. With its sturdy accordion fold-outs, Day and Night First Words is the perfect tummy-time book for your newborn. On the day side of the book your baby will follow the routine of a happy polar bear cub as he eats and plays his day away. On the reverse side of the accordion fold, the cub bathes and gets ready for bed. The high-contrast shapes and patterns in Day and Night provide your baby with something simple and engaging to focus on during the so-important tummy time.

Scheduling
For infants, do tummy time daily until they begin crawling. Day and Night First Words is a great companion for this activity, or swap in other dynamically contrasting books or toys for variety. For toddlers, place Day and Night First Words in your library of choices for your daily reading routine.

LET'S SIGN, BABY!

INFANT ~ ~~TODDLER~~ ~ TINY TOTS ELITE

Communication doesn't have to wait until your baby can speak. Why not start much earlier? We have been ASL advocates ever since we saw firsthand the benefits of teaching sign language to a baby. Babies that can communicate their needs tend to be less frustrated, speak earlier, have a wider vocabulary, and often go on to have a higher-than-average literacy level.

Let's Sign, Baby! is a gentle, natural way to reinforce the benefits of ASL with your baby. Using simple stories, your baby will follow three children through a well-chosen daily activity that your baby can relate to—making it fascinating to read, rewarding to sign, and easy to remember.

One page of each two-page spread in Let's Sign, Baby! is devoted to demonstrating a word or two that is pertinent to the storyline. It's the ideal interactive activity book for this age!

Scheduling
Because it is both interactive and a story, this book can be read many times a week, or until the signs are learned by both of you.

MY FIRST BABY SIGNS

INFANT ~ ~~TODDLER~~ ~ TINY TOTS ELITE

Many of the foster babies we have welcomed into our home spent much of the initial days screaming because we couldn't understand what they wanted. That is why one of our first courses of action was to teach them basic sign language. My First Baby Signs has been designed to bridge the gap between what baby knows he wants and what he can say. With pull tabs to demonstrate how to make eight different signs, My First Baby Signs will help your baby make the connections between the words and the actions, and bright, colorful graphics will appeal to baby. Even though the use of tabbed movements is ingenious, My First Baby Signs is not a book that will withstand little unsupervised bumbling fingers, so this is a book you'll read together, and then put away for next time.

Scheduling the Pre-Verbal Child
You'll want to read My First Baby Signs with your child frequently during the months that signing is your baby's primary communication method. We recommend reading it three to five times a week to reinforce the signs that you're using in everyday life.

Scheduling the Verbal Child
Place My First Baby Signs in your library of choices for your reading routine.

ABC BABY SIGNS

~~INFANT~~ **TODDLER ~ TINY TOTS ELITE**

Give your little ones a pedagogical advantage by teaching them how to communicate with their hands. ABC Baby Signs uses the alphabet as a springboard to familiarize your baby with 26 practical, useful, and baby-friendly words in sign language. Accompanying each word is a short bit of prose that describes the gestures of that word.

The ethnically-diverse images are lively and engaging, while insets at the top of each page demonstrate the appropriate sign in a simple diagram. As a bonus, there are an additional four pages of everyday signs to round out this charming collection.

Scheduling the Pre-Signing Child
Once baby is ready to get started, begin by simply choosing a couple of new words every week to learn. By six months, you can help your baby make simple signs by assisting him hand-over-hand. The really fun part is that this is the age where signing really starts to click for you and your baby. Yes, even this early! Mealtime is ideal to begin working on signs in earnest. We like to start with something like: "Milk!" The emerging communication is always such a highlight—enjoy!

Scheduling the Beginning-to-Sign Child
Keep building his repertoire of signs. He can control his hands better than his words, so the more signs you both know, the more he'll be able to communicate to you. Plus, signing helps rather than hinders speech, as it actually helps him learn more words!

Very First Book of Things to Spot

~~INFANT~~ **TODDLER ~ TINY TOTS ELITE**

Watch your baby's language comprehension explode with Very First Book of Things to Spot, Very First Book of Things to Spot at Home, and Very First Book of Things to Spot Out and About. Searching the simple, beautifully-illustrated pages, your baby will learn the names of items and their adjectives as you discuss sizes, clothing, colors, activities, and more.

Linger on a page or read through an entire book, whatever holds the interest of both you and your baby. Just doing a page or two a day will enrich your baby's vocabulary in a way that you both will find enjoyable. Each page has several suggested questions, and you undoubtedly will come up with dozens more.

Scheduling
Read to your baby from each of the three books once a week, or more if desired.

MOTOR SKILLS

LET'S GET MOVING!
From that first grasp of your finger to when his unsteady steps turn into a sprint, your baby's motor skills will improve during these years. From grasping and reaching to vestibular stimulation, the next tools will help set your baby in motion.

BUMPIE GERTIE BALL

INFANT ~ ~~TODDLER~~ ~ TINY TOTS ELITE

Throwing and catching will help improve your baby's coordination and dexterity skills. One of the best baby balls is the specially textured Bumpie Gertie Ball. With its soft, baby-friendly knobs and its squishy, slightly sticky texture, the Bumpie Gertie Ball is super easy to catch and throw. Babies love the squeezable bumps and easy-to-grasp feel, while parents appreciate that Bumpie Gertie Balls are always light and gentle, which makes them ideal for indoor play.

Scheduling Infancy
Use the Bumpie Gertie Ball to add interest to tummy time, and occasionally have your baby hold it or run it gently over his body to experience sensory input. However, it is not a teething toy.

Scheduling 6 – 18 months
Use the Bumpie Gertie Ball several times a week. Your baby can gradually learn to creep toward it, crawl to it, push it, sit and "catch" it when rolled, and throw it.

Scheduling Older Toddlers
Practice your older toddler's catching and kicking skills. The small size of the Bumpie Gertie Ball means it requires more precision than the larger Gertie Ball. Use Bumpie Gertie Ball several times a week until skill proficiency, then for free play as desired.

PEANUT BALL

INFANT ~ ~~TODDLER~~ ~ TINY TOTS ELITE

Unless you've read Active Baby, Healthy Brain, the idea of a peanut exercise ball may seem baffling. But the author explains how an exercise and therapy ball, with its inclination towards instability, will strengthen your baby's core muscles, body awareness, balance, and attention.

You can use any exercise ball, but we like the idea of using The Amazing Peanut Ball. Because of its unique shape, it will roll in only one direction, so the instability is moderate, making it a lot less daunting for new parents to use.

The center of the Peanut Ball will hold any rider safely within its contoured "saddle," so don't be surprised to find that this Peanut Ball morphs into a trusty steed for older siblings when baby is napping. Eye-hand and brain coordination are greatly enhanced by vestibular stimulation, so start early and encourage his developing brain.

Scheduling 0-6 Months
Vestibular stimulation is so important, and rocking your baby gently on the Peanut Ball is a great way to help him learn to organize the sensory input he receives all day long. Try deflating the ball some for the very young baby, and always, always keep safety first.

Scheduling 6-12 Months
As your baby gets stronger, gently increase the intensity of his "workout" to keep it at a level that is fun and interesting to him. Never get wild with him, though; not only is his brain fragile, but you also don't want to scare him.

Scheduling 12 Months and Up
Vestibular stimulation is just as important as ever, so make sure you work it in every day. Try moving to the rhythm of your favorite music or making up a song to go along with your actions. As always, keep safety first!

GERTIE BALL
~~INFANT~~ **TODDLER ~ TINY TOTS ELITE**

Rolling, throwing, catching, and kicking are all skills that will improve your little one's coordination and dexterity. One of the best balls for the littles is the specially-textured Gertie Ball. With its squishy, slightly-sticky, very huggable texture, the Gertie Ball is super easy to catch and throw. Everyone loves the easy-to-grasp, gummy feel, while parents appreciate that Gertie Balls are always light and gentle. The larger Gertie Balls can be inflated to various sizes and used at various skill levels, then deflated easily for traveling. Safe for all ages, although parental supervision is recommended to ensure your child doesn't try to chew the ball or play with the air plug.

Scheduling Babies
Gertie Ball integrates well into some Active Baby, Healthy Brain activities. During playtime, older babies who are crawling and sitting can learn to easily roll the Gertie Ball and catch it when it is rolled to them.

Scheduling Toddlers
The size of the Gertie Ball makes it a bit cumbersome for young babies to catch, but for toddlers, it shines. Gertie Ball's larger size makes it a superb tool to teach young toddlers rudimentary catching and kicking skills. We recommend using it several times a week until some proficiency is achieved, then "graduating" to the smaller Bumpie Gertie Ball for a greater challenge.

Scheduling Older Toddlers
If you're looking for fun active games for older toddlers, Gertie Ball lends itself well to basketball (with a box or wastepaper can on a chair), bowling (with empty or slightly-filled water bottles), soccer (with a box tipped on its side), and innumerable other toddler sports. Besides expending energy, these activities will develop hand-eye coordination, motor planning, reflexes, and, depending on what you play, the important life skills of sportsmanship and taking turns.

CATERPILLAR STACKING

~~INFANT~~ — **TODDLER ~ TINY TOTS ELITE**

At this age, your focus will be finding toys that target fine motor skills, and if they develop sorting, matching, and sequencing skills, so much the better. Caterpillar Stacking, with its chubby, smoothly rounded, tactilely rich shapes, answers that need. Ideal for toddlers, Caterpillar Stacking segments can be assembled and reassembled on its gorgeous solid wood-pegged base to create a variety of colorful caterpillars. Your 18-month-old toddler will love the challenge of just stacking the colorful pieces on the pegs. As time goes on, you can encourage him to put all the similarly hued colors together. Later still, slip one of the very sturdy pattern cards into the all-wood holder and he can copy the pattern of the caterpillars depicted. Caterpillar Stacking develops color recognition and discrimination, sequencing, sensory exploration, manipulative skills, and critical reasoning.

Scheduling 12 – 24 months
Your one-year-old will enjoy the challenge of placing pieces on the pegs – this makes a great highchair activity to avoid the risk of unsteady walkers falling on the pegs. Some children will not be interested in Caterpillar Stacking at 12 months. Don't push it, but keep bringing it out until they are ready. At that point, aim to play with Caterpillar Stacking once or twice a week.

Scheduling the Advanced Child
As your child incrementally learns to match the cards, Caterpillar Stacking becomes a superb puzzle to use two or more times a week.

PALETTE OF PEGS
~~INFANT~~ **TODDLER ~ TINY TOTS ELITE**

Loved by occupational therapists, parents, and children alike, Palette of Pegs will develop and strengthen visual perception skills, hand-eye coordination, and fine motor skills, including the pincer grasp. It's such an amazing workout for little hands! With its rainbow of colors, Palette of Pegs is one of the most versatile pegboards for toddlers. Use it to develop color recognition, sorting, and sequencing skills. Match the ring to the peg or go color-crazy. Then try stacking the pegs with the rings–can the stacked rings keep it stable? Heirloom-quality Palette of Pegs' brilliant colors come from solvent-free paints, so there is never any worry when toys wander from hand to mouth.

A toddler will spend a lot of time touching stuff, which is an activity where the eyes tell the brain that there is something that looks interesting and to engage the hands to find out more. However, the eyes will not necessarily stay focused on the object that is being picked up unless there is a reason. Therefore, there is a need to give your toddler specific activities where the eyes need to stay focused in order to guide little hands to successfully complete an activity. Working with Palette of Pegs will give your toddler a chance to work on hand-eye coordination, visual focusing, and tracking skills, all of which are vital skills.

From pincer grasp, tripod grasp, grasp and release, thumb opposition, and bilateral hand coordination to hand-eye coordination, visual discrimination, and visual motor planning, Palette of Pegs yields endless benefits.

Since children learn to take things out before they learn to put them in, use Palette of Pegs and have your child remove each peg and place it in a container. Once his grasp and release skill is well developed, help him master inserting the peg back in the board. Next, children will begin to isolate the thumb and first two fingers to pick up and release things. Palette of Pegs will aid the development of this "tripod grasp." Finally, the most challenging grasp of all is the pincer grasp, picking up small pegs using the thumb and index finger in opposition. As your child's skills progress, Palette of Pegs can be used to develop other skills.

Scheduling
Beginning as soon as your baby is ready, at around 10 months old, play with Palette of Pegs often–about twice a week is a reasonable goal. You might have your baby develop skills in the following sequence:

Phase 1:
Allow your child to remove the pegs.

Phase 2:
Encourage him to remove the pegs and put them in a container. (Be forewarned, this age loves putting things in and out of containers!)

Phase 3:
Help your child to place the pegs in the board, either a few or all of them. Hand-over-hand assistance often helps this click for your child.

Phase 4:
Your child is now ready to place both the pegs and rings on the board.

Phase 5:
Now your child is ready for the most challenging version, placing rings on color-matching pegs. Starting with a couple of obviously different colors at a time is very helpful, then just work up to more and more until he can do the entire board.

Bonus Activity: Can your child build a tower with rings and pegs? How tall can he make it?

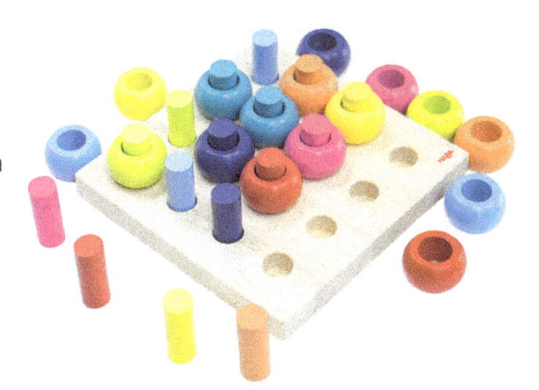

Poke-A-Dot Popper
~~INFANT~~ **TODDLER ~ TINY TOTS ELITE**

This one-of-a-kind popping toy will develop your child's fine motor skills, hand-eye coordination, and auditory processing as he pops each bubble.

The buttons in the Poke-A-Dot Poppers can be popped repeatedly, and the rugged wooden Popper comes with a convenient Velcro loop to hang on a stroller.

Each Popper side is different and so is the sound that it makes.

Your toddler is going to enjoy the pictures and the sturdy feel of this wooden tool. But the little bubbles to pop will be his favorite and he won't even notice the effort he's putting into getting one finger in place to pop each one!

Scheduling for Toddlers
Ideally your child will have access to this tool at least twice a week. Some parents will prefer to keep it as a special car toy to make trips less tedious, others will strap it to the stroller, toddler carrier, or toss it in the "school" bin.

Pop Toobs

~~INFANT~~ — **TODDLER ~ TINY TOTS ELITE**

For the price, this is one of the most versatile toys your family can own. We loved them over 20 years ago, and were recently reintroduced to them when our foster toddler needed occupational therapy. Pop Toobs are amazing! Kids universally love the cool sound and vibrating sensation they make when Pop Toobs are extended. Pop Toobs can be popped, stretched, bent, and connected together, providing tactile stimulation, fine motor skills, and auditory feedback (they make a satisfying sound with each movement). Use it as a bugle and annoy the family pet, practice fine motor skills by fitting marshmallows in them, pretend to be a scuba diver and bubble in the tub, or bend one into a "C" and listen to your voice. In therapy, Pop Toobs improve bilateral coordination, hand and finger strength, sensory output, and provide great auditory and tactile stimulation. In your home, these bendable, connectable tubes provide hours of fun play.

Scheduling
Pop Toobs are fairly lightweight, so our recommendation would be to only get one out at a time and consider them disposable when your baby's enthusiasm takes its unavoidable toll. With so many activities, Pop Toobs can be used about twice a week, or more if you'd like.

Activities for 8 months and older
1. Send Cheerios or other safe foods down a Pop Toob chute, reinforcing object permanency and baby-level physics.
2. Extend the Pop Toobs.
3. Let him hear his own voice with a C-shaped "phone" for speech readiness.
4. Play whisper phone, as you hold one end of a Pop Toob to his ear and the other end to your mouth (check your volume on yourself first, so as not to overwhelm his ears).

Additional activities for toddlers
1. Collapsing the Pop Toob.
2. Snapping two or more Pop Toobs together.
3. Integrating Pop Toobs into imaginary play.

STEM

STEM IS EVERYWHERE!

STEM learning is more than robotics and computer programming. STEM tools also include those that engage students in exploratory learning, discovery, and problem solving that teach the foundational skills of critical thinking and short- and long-term planning. So STEM includes your Miffy Hide & Seek set as well as your Caterpillar Stacking logic game and your Pop Toobs, even though they are listed elsewhere in this handbook. Basically anything that goes beyond a rote read-and-regurgitate lesson undoubtedly falls into the STEM classification. In assembling this guide, many of our products could easily have been classified as STEM, but these three tools seem especially appropriate for this category.

STACKABLE FOREST
~~INFANT~~ — **TODDLER ~ TINY TOTS ELITE**

Mushroom, and tree, and bear – oh my! All toddlers love to stack, and now they can have fun and create their own forest, complete with adorable bear. The Stackable Forest is loaded with opportunities for you to engage your toddler in language about colors, animal parts, and even positional words like bottom/middle/top.

The eight wooden pieces, all water painted in forest colors, are stacked to form the bear, mushroom, and pine tree. Each chunky stacking shape has pegs or holes to keep the stacked figures in place.

The Stackable Forest develops size recognition, stacking skills, manipulative skills, and hand-eye coordination.

Scheduling
From 8 - 12 months old, your child will mostly be doing freeplay with the Stackable Forest. He'll begin with unstacking the forest, then graduate to occasionally stacking them accidentally at first, and then intentionally. With no long center peg, this is one of the safest stacking toys available.

Later, coach your toddler to build the bear, mushroom, or tree using the specific pieces. As with any set, you can scaffold this heavily at first by putting pieces he doesn't need out of reach, and handing him only the one he needs next. Make sure to cheer him on!

If you'd like to work on auditory directions/colors then have him hand you the piece you need. "May I have the white one? Thank you! Next we need that red piece..."

GRIPPIES SHAKERS
~~INFANT~~ **TODDLER ~ TINY TOTS ELITE**

The Grippies Shakers set is both a collection of rattles and a multifaceted magnetic construction kit. Connect the chunky, colorful, easy-to-grasp magnetic rods to each other or combine them with the coated metal ball connectors to create a secure, frustration-free introduction to building.

Toddlers can watch the sensory beads rattle their way down the magnetic rods over a variety of shapes that produce a range of soft sounds.

Grippies Shakers is a versatile, intellectually-stimulating construction set that will test your children's dexterity as well as their creative thinking skills, and it is perfect for toddlers to develop their auditory skills, fine and gross motor skills, and engineering skills.

Scheduling 0-10 months
You won't really use Grippies Shakers as construction tools for a while, but right now you can use them as rattles, toys for your baby to chew on and explore, or even as towers for him to knock down.

Scheduling 10-12 months
As he gets more mobile, he will thoroughly enjoy knocking towers over and pulling pieces apart. But it won't be long now until he's building his own towers.

Scheduling 12 months and up
Show him how pieces stick together and start using the enclosed booklet for ideas on simple patterns he can duplicate. Here are several more ideas:

1. Crash!
Have baby knock the tower down with his hands.

2. Bowling
Try knocking a tower over by "bowling" for it. Or you can build your tower on a blanket, then pull it until the tower falls.

3. Build Towers
Yep, it's as simple as it sounds!

4. Fence Them In
Fence in your toy animals. Put them all in one big enclosure, or divide them up by type of animal and naturally work on sorting.

5. Build a Match
Have your toddler match what you build. Start very simply– just join a couple of pieces together and coach him every step of the way. "My first piece is green. Find a green piece!" "I'm putting on a white ball. Put a white ball piece on yours!"

6. Skyscrapers
Build the tallest tower possible with your toddler, helping him reach to place the last pieces.

7. Colors
You can teach colors with Grippies Shakers! When building a multi-colored tower, talk about each piece's color. "Do you want the orange one?" "I'm going to put a yellow one on." Point out color similarities, too. "This blue one is the same color as your shirt!"

8. Sorting by Color
Have your toddler sort the blocks by color.

9. What Size Is It?
Now have him sort the blocks by size and by shape. This will be a perfect opportunity to introduce the vocabulary of bigger and smaller. This will not be the only place you'll want to introduce size or color language since each color corresponds to a size (e.g., blue pieces are always long) instead of being assorted. However, it is a very practical place to use the vocabulary and familiarize your child with the concepts.

10. Count
Introduce counting by coaching your toddler to hand you one piece, two pieces, etc.

11. First, Second, Third…
Work on other math vocabulary, such as, "Put this piece on second" or "Should we add a third piece?"

12. Comparisons
Build towers of different sizes while talking about measurement and placement vocabulary. "The tower in front is wider than the tower behind," and "This tower is taller than our first tower."

13. Measure It
As your child approaches two, you can begin to introduce measurement by using pieces as units of measure. How many rods long is your toddler's arm? How long is your arm? Can you measure how wide your chair is?

14. Patterns
Practice patterns by setting up a repeating pattern of colors, such as blue – red – blue – red – blue, and ask your child to place the next piece.

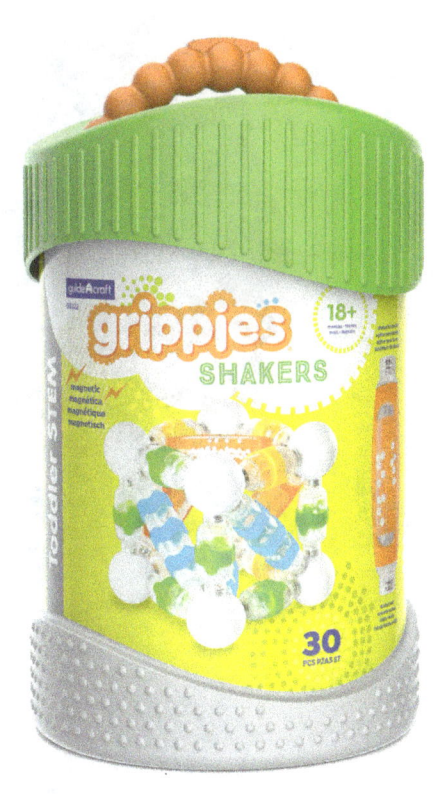

3-D Shape Sorter
~~INFANT~~ **TODDLER ~ TINY TOTS ELITE**

The soft, squishy, and downy-to-touch Rubbabu 3-D Animal Shape Sorter is a perfect first puzzle for younger children. From 8 to 24 months, when children are too young for puzzles with small pieces, they are still ready to learn animal shapes and colors.

Even the tiniest of children can pick up, examine, and play with the nine brightly colored shapes, then with a gentle push place them back in their soft base. The seriously soft, velvety surface offers tactile stimulation.

Handmade of natural rubber foam, the Rubbabu 3-D Animal Shape Sorter is anti-microbial, dust-mite resistant, mildew resistant, hypo-allergenic, and flame resistant, but it is not a teething toy. Because these items are handmade, variations and slight imperfections are normal, and are part of the character of the product.

Scheduling
Babies as young as 8 months old will enjoy clutching these velvety shapes, and they may even like helping you pat them into place in the Shape Sorter. Gradually over the next year, help them learn to solve this puzzle on their own. While the Shape Sorter may be too difficult for even a two-year-old on his first try, with repeated, gradual practice it can be achieved by even your younger toddler.

As your toddler's skills develop, we suggest a goal of working on a puzzle as part of his daily routine three to five times a week. Choose any of the puzzles in our curriculum (including Palette of Pegs and Stackable Forest), or rotate in your favorite family hand-me-downs.

SOCIAL SKILLS

SOLVING PROBLEMS, PLAYING TOGETHER
These four tools teach very different social aspects, which is why together they are invaluable. The Wimmer-Ferguson Baby Mirror teaches self-awareness and imitation skills, in addition to many others. By reading (and practicing!) the faces in Making Faces your baby will be learning to identify and express emotions. Wee Baby Stella is amazing for teaching problem solving, recognition of the feelings of others, and so many fine motor skills. Miffy Hide & Seek may be your child's very first peer game, and teaches so many skills, from good sportsmanship to auditory processing. Plus, it's a ton of fun!

WIMMER - FERGUSON BABY MIRROR

INFANT ~ ~~TODDLER~~ ~ TINY TOTS ELITE

Babies love to look at faces, and that is a good thing for their development. With a mirror you can boost your baby's hand-eye coordination, language, listening, and imitation skills. The Oppenheim Toy Portfolio says that there is not a better quality safety mirror for babies than the Wimmer-Ferguson Baby Mirror, and we are in agreement.

The Wimmer-Ferguson Baby Mirror is much more distortion-free than typical toy mirrors. Plus, on the reverse of the mirror are visually stimulating black and white graphics for your baby to gaze at.

Baby-safe and shatter-proof, it measures 14" x 10", with ribbon ties for easy attachment.

Scheduling
You're going to want to use this early and often with your little one. Grab it for tummy time, set it at the changing table, or hang it on the outside of his crib. (Nothing inside the crib for safe sleep, of course.) He may also love it for car time - but keep an eye on him to see if it's making him motionsick or if the sunlight is reflecting off of it into his eyes.

Don't forget to use the reverse side as well, particularly in baby's early weeks when high-contrast images help him develop his ocular muscles.

~~G~~ FACES: A FIRST BOOK OF EMOTIONS

~~INFANT~~ **TODDLER ~ TINY TOTS ELITE**

~~intro~~duction to five common emotions, Making ~~Firs~~t Book of Emotions is a wonderfully interactive ~~for b~~abies and toddlers. A beautiful board book, ~~Making F~~aces presents the most familiar baby emotions: ~~happy,~~ sad, angry, surprised, and silly.

~~On t~~he left-hand page, Making Faces uses large photographs ~~of a s~~ingle child's face on a white background to provide ~~maxi~~mum contrast and to help babies zero in on facial ~~expr~~essions. On the facing page, your baby is asked to find ~~the s~~ame face ~~amon~~g photos ~~showi~~ng all five ~~emotion~~s. The ~~pictur~~e in ~~Making F~~aces ~~allows a~~ mirror ~~so you~~ and ~~baby~~ can ~~see m~~aking ~~face~~s.

As he gets older, he will start pointing to the match on his own.

As soon as he masters that, start asking him to find a different face than the text suggests - for instance, on the page below, having him find a sad, happy, angry, or silly face.

And don't forget to use the mirror. It's so much fun to watch a baby master facial expressions!

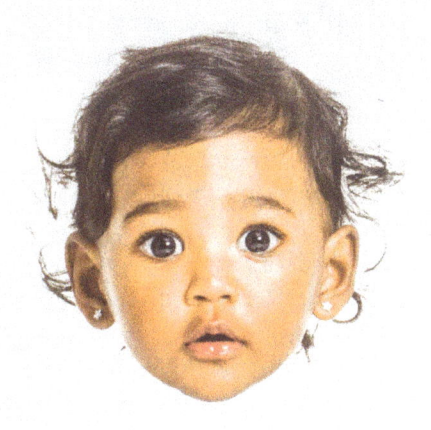

Look at the **SURPRISED** baby.

Can you make a **SURPRISED** face?

Find the **SURPRISED** baby!

2018-2019 Tiny Tots Curriculum Handbook • 800.478.0672   121

WEE BABY STELLA

~~INFANT~~ **TODDLER ~ TINY TOTS ELITE**

Empathy, recognizing the feelings of others and responding with care, is a very complex social-emotional skill for a toddler to develop. Roleplaying with dolls is an excellent way to enact and reenact different scenarios. Wee Baby Stella will allow you to demonstrate to your child that others may have different feelings than he has and how to respond to them. Maybe a pacifier for fussiness, a bottle for hunger, or a toy for boredom.

The super-cuddly 12" Wee Baby Stella is a perfect companion for practicing fine motor skills, responsibility, nurturing, and caring. Wee Baby Stella releases a soothing lavender scent, perfect for calming your toddler. Wee Baby Stella can be surface washed only, and is not for us[e as a] toy under the age of one.

Scheduling

From about 8 months old, your baby can parti[cipate and] mimic your actions as you care for Wee Baby [Stella. By] 18 months old, your toddler can take the lea[d with Wee Baby] Stella. Dressing and undressing Wee Baby S[tella,] as needed, will practice the developmental [skills needed] for your child to dress and undress himsel[f. Engage] in imitative play with Wee Baby Stella at l[east three] times a week, reenacting scenarios that a[re part of his] experience.

MIFFY HIDE & SEEK
~~INFANT~~ **TODDLER ~ TINY TOTS ELITE**

Miffy Hide & Seek allows you to engage in this brain-boosting event without taking your eyes off your child. Just hide Miffy and listen for her cheerful "I am here! I am here!" that sounds every 10 seconds. Use only her voice or a combination of her chirps and the clue cards to direct your child to finding her. When you use the clue cards, your toddler's listening, observation, and following directions skills are strengthened.

Miffy Hide & Seek can also be used to help your toddler strengthen his emotional and cognitive development through play. Thinking of hiding places or trying to find Miffy forces your child to be strategic and use his imagination. Plus, hide and seek has even been proven to teach children volume and the concept of size and spaces. From a social perspective, Miffy Hide & Seek is a great forum for practicing turn-taking skills, as well as learning how to work as part of a team and how to handle both victory and defeat. Lastly, there are well-known physical benefits that can be seen as your toddler searches, such as coordination, balance, and agility.

Scheduling
Beginning when your baby is young, hide Miffy under the Playsilk while your baby watches, then let him tug the silk off to find her. Gradually increase the difficulty by hiding her when baby is not watching, and in a variety of places. You can use the sound only, or the sound and clues in tandem. When your toddler is older, you can use multiple clue cards to create a type of treasure hunt. Play with Miffy Hide & Seek as often as you'd like; we suggest once a week or more.

...have shown that hide and seek, a game we ...h early childhood, profoundly influences ...elopment. For infants and young toddlers, that ... toys in front of them so they can seek them; ...erfect for that.

...months through 3 years, start by hiding ...easy locations and letting them find her. ..., Miffy Hide & Seek helps with problem ...d attention maintenance. Attention ...bility of the child to focus without

SENSORY

CAN YOU FEEL THAT?

According to Janet Doman, one of the authors of How Smart Is Your Baby?, "a newborn ba[by] is functionally blind, deaf and insensate." She believes that it is up to the parents to use se[nsory] stimulation to develop the sensory pathways that lead to proper brain development and [...] Using positive sensory stimulation (through all five senses) in brief intervals will help the [...] pathways to become strong, and therefore, will achieve a sense of permanent learning[.]

Researchers believe that beginning at about three months, babies need intentional se[nsory] stimulation in order to nurture intellectual growth, and that if we address it early en[ough] prevent the all-encompassing and debilitating functional impact that sensory proce[ssing] can have on a child.

There are countless ways to do that, and these five tools are just a start. Make sur[e to work] many sensory experiences into daily life as is possible–from stroking velvet to dig[ging] and squashing mud pies.

STARRY NIGHT PLAYSILK
INFANT ~ ~~TODDLER~~ ~ TINY TOTS ELITE

Simple and natural, Playsilks have been recommended for nearly 100 years to encourage children to use their imagination and creativity. The sumptuously soft feel of Playsilks is ideal for developing babies. Wispy enough for a tiny baby to manipulate, Playsilks provide a wonderful sensory experience. They are great for "peek-a-boo," and the lovely texture and translucency of the Playsilk make it ideal for "hiding and finding" games with your baby. Easily stuffed into a diaper bag or purse, Playsilks make a soft, filmy, easy-to-pack "comfy" for traveling little ones.

As your babies grow, so does the versatility of their Playsilk. Little girls can become princesses and little boys, dragon-slayers. Wrap a baby doll, hoist a flag, or set the table for a tea party; there are unlimited hours of open-ended play with a Playsilk.

Silk is remarkably durable and can withstand years of play. We recommend hand washing with warm water and a mild soap, then drying in a dryer set on low for a few minutes to restore the softness and remove wrinkles. For some reason, many children enjoy washing their Playsilks and hanging them outside to dry. It is a wonderfully peaceful experience, so let them do this often!

Scheduling
Unlimited!

pipSquigz Loops
INFANT ~ ~~TODDLER~~ ~ TINY TOTS ELITE

Because sensory development is a crucial component of your baby's healthy development, you need pipSquigz Loops. Combining touch, sound, and visual stimulation, the two smart, take-anywhere pipSquigz Loops are perfect for the stroller, high chair, bathtub, and just about anywhere else. pipSquigz Loops are colorful, bendy, and chewy! Your baby can spin the textured plastic rings to hear the sweet jingle, but they are also great for teething and for developing motor skills.

You can push pipSquigz Loops down on any smooth surface and watch your baby tug, push, and shake them. Or, suction the two pipSquigz Loops together for an additional play experience. Compact and sized to take anywhere, pipSquigz Loops are easy to clean and totally safe for teething babies.

Scheduling
Use pipSquigz Loops as a wonderful rattle and teether during your child's early development. As he begins sitting independently, start using them on his high chair, the sliding glass door, the floor, or wherever else will keep his attention and build his muscles as he tries to remove/bend them.

YOEE BABY

~ ~~TODDLER~~ ~ **TINY TOTS ELITE**

Science tells us that playful interactions in the ve[...] months of your baby's life have a lasting impact o[...] architecture of his developing brain and will lay a f[...] for all future learning and behavior. Engaging your [...] can actually change the way your baby's brain deve[...] Yoee Baby considered your baby's developing sense[...] and brain synapses (which are, at that age, forming by [...] hour), and designed a toy that includes interaction and [...] bonding, sensory development, body awareness, langu[...] development, gross motor skills, and fine motor skills. W[...] parents are often eager to engage their little one from th[...] moment of birth, it is difficult to find a toy that is not only [...] safe but actually promotes early bonding. Yoee Baby not only encourages parents and babies to play together in ways that nurture those bonds, but also strengthens early childhood development skills.

Not just for moms and dads, the uber-cute Yoee Baby characters' soft, feather-like tail, designed to caress baby and stimulate his senses, also provides an ideal way for your other children to attach to their new sibling. One of the hardest things a child, especially a toddler, faces is figuring out how he can interact with this baby who isn't grasping, crawling, talking, or doing anything that could be considered interactive. But with Yoee Baby your child can, by tickling the baby with the feather-like tail, begin to make that all-important connection. Bonding isn't something that comes naturally or instinctively to many younger children, but from day one Yoee Baby will help them build that skill.

Not only can your baby be gently caressed with the long fluffy tail, the crinkle high-contrast fabrics and rattle inside of a Yoee Baby are another fun way to engage baby's senses. The handle is designed so that both babies and adults can easily hold and play with a Yoee Baby, plus the food-grade

2018-2019 Tiny Tots Curriculum Handbook

MAKING

A simple introd[...] Faces: A Firs[...] book for h[...] Making [...] happy.[...]

On t[...] of a s[...] maxi[...] expr[...] the s[...] amon[...] showi[...] feeling[...] last pag[...] Making [...] includes [...] where yo[...] your baby[...] practice ma[...] your own faw[...]

Sch[...] Unli[...] putti[...] list if a[...] your c[...] it just b[...] whateve[...] get into a[...] from the s[...]

[...] attached to the [...] can be a relief [...] And don't forget [...] rable plush Yoee [...] a story prop to [...] y all sorts of wild [...] timulate language [...] ent. While each Yoee [...] hes with a simple [...] booklet, there's no [...] wrong way to use your [...] by as long as you and [...] having fun.

[...] by social scientists, [...] is made for babies [...] hs and combines [...] plush toy, a [...] nd sensory [...] d a rattle [...] by toy for [...] Machine [...] air dry. [...] [...] [...]

Scheduling
For a tiny little one just read the book as written and help baby point to the answers.

127

TAGGIES CRINKLE
INFANT ~ ~~TODDLER~~ ~ TINY TOTS ELITE

Taggies Crinkle Heather Hedgehog will stimulate your baby's senses and give his cognitive development a jump-start. Language development in babies is triggered by toys that make sounds. Heather Hedgehog is a safe, crinkly, crackly toy especially made for babies' auditory as well as sensory development. This is why baby toys rattle, jingle, or squeak.

One of the sounds most universally loved by babies is the crinkly sound that paper makes. Yet in most homes, because paper can be messy and there is the risk of babies choking on it, it is often taken away. But Taggies Crinkle is a safe, cute, fun alternative.

Not just for auditory development, Taggies Crinkle is also beneficial for sensory development. Chewable and twistable, with Heather Hedgehog you will never have to worry about pokes or paper cuts. Super soft and light as a feather, Heather Hedgehog is just the right size for tiny fingers to hold and squeeze; the squeaker inside adds to the sensory fun.

Heather Hedgehog can also double as a teether. When your baby reaches and grabs for the eight interactive and soothing satin loop tags, he's also developing his fine motor skills, as well as his hand-eye coordination, and he's receiving the tactile stimulation that babies crave. Includes a flexible loop for attaching to stroller and car seat.

Scheduling
Introduce this to baby as soon as he seems interested, probably about 3 months old. We like to save ours for times when we can't interact with him as much as we'd like - whether that's a long car ride, or helping a sibling in the bathroom. The Taggies Crinkle is a fun distraction that teaches so many skills while keeping baby happy.

TACTILE SEARCH AND MATCH

~~INFANT~~ TODDLER ~ TINY TOTS ELITE

Toddlers will learn best and retain more information when they engage their senses while learning. Sensory play is crucial to brain development as it builds nerve connections in the brain's pathways and supports cognitive growth, language development, gross motor skills, and more. Sensory play is also great for quieting a fearful or frustrated toddler.

Tactile Search and Match is a sensory puzzle for toddlers. Feel and identify matching pieces from their bumpy ridges, smooth surfaces, soft plush exteriors, and more. Nine different textures on oversized rubberwood puzzle pieces match to a corresponding spot on the sturdy puzzle board.

Practice color and pattern identification with this engaging, tactile matching game. The sturdy puzzle board has overmolded handles for easy mobility.

Scheduling
As soon as your child is able to manipulate the pieces, you can begin playing with this set. Here are some ideas for you, roughly in order of difficulty:

Phase 1:
Remove all the pieces from the board.

Phase 2:
Put the pieces back into the puzzle - anywhere.

Phase 3:
Put the pieces in the right spot on the board as you call them out. "Next, let's match this soft white one. Can you find the soft white piece to put on top?"

Phase 4:
Put all the pieces back independently. (To work up to this one, try giving him one or two pieces at a time, then three or four, etc.)

Phase 5:
Use it like a memory game. This is a tricky way to play, but perfect if your tiny one has an older sibling itching to take a turn with it. Flip all nine puzzle pieces over so that all you can see is the wooden back. Then pick a piece you're trying to fill in on the board: "I'm fishing for the blue wavy piece," and flip over a piece to see if it matches. If so, you keep the piece and play again. If not, flip it back and the other person gets a turn to play.

Phase 6:
As a variation on the last game, place the pieces into a pillowcase or other opaque bag instead of flipping them over. When it's your turn, announce which piece you will be fishing for, then feel around in the bag until you find it. If you were right, keep the piece, but if not, throw it back in. Either way, pass the play to the next person so no one person wins them all.

DEVELOPMENTAL PLAY

IT'S MORE THAN JUST PLAY TIME

For your infant, Developmental Play is the heart of thinking skills, spatial awareness, motor skills, regulation, and so much more. These tools are all designed for your baby to begin using before his first birthday - though we expect them to be useful longer than that.

You'll notice an emphasis on soothing a teething baby - but those tools are the exact same ones that work on the motor skills, self-soothing, eye-hand coordination, spatial awareness, and so much more. Is it ever "just" a toy at this age?

AMBER AND WOOD TEETHING RING

INFANT ~ ~~TODDLER~~ ~ TINY TOTS ELITE

When babies are teething, they put everything into their mouths trying to soothe their aching gums. For some babies, particularly older ones, rubber teethers can be too soft and pliable. But wooden teethers, like the Heimess Amber and Wood Teething Ring, is not only durable and toxin-free, but will give your baby a different, less malleable surface to gnaw on.

The Amber and Wood Teething Ring is perfect for the parent who prefers untreated wooden teethers from sustainable indigenous forests, and is especially suitable for babies with allergies and immune deficiencies. Made in Germany for more than 50 years, the Amber and Wood Teething Ring is a great way for babies to explore shapes and textures and makes a lovely sound when shaken.

Scheduling
Use as desired for those seemingly endless teething days or just for beautiful variety in the toybox.

BOLLI

INFANT ~ ~~TODDLER~~ ~ TINY TOTS ELITE

Made of food-grade silicone, Bolli is a flexible ball for your infant to explore with his hands or his mouth. Bolli can be stretched, squished, and gummed, and because of its open-ball design it is easy for babies to hang on to.

Scheduling
This is easy to schedule. Whenever your tiny baby is fussy and in need of a teether, hand him his Bolli!

GERTIE THE GOOD GOOSE

INFANT ~ ~~TODDLER~~ ~ TINY TOTS ELITE

Reduce and alleviate teething pain with the all-natural Gertie the Good Goose. The combination of soft and hard plastics enables your baby to use the various textures as a form of relief from throbbing gums. Gertie has been expertly sized to fit perfectly in babies' hands and to soothe tender gums.

Velvety to the touch, Gertie has a slight vanilla scent, and she has contrasting colors making her easier for babies to focus on. Babies especially love Gertie's soulful gaze.

So lightweight, and with simple contours, Gertie is effortless for your baby to grasp and manipulate freely. And she makes a cute squeak when squeezed, providing sensory awareness and teaching your baby cause and effect.

Scheduling
Fantastic for auditory/visual tracking, early grasping skills, and of course teething and playing, we suggest making this a regular part of your little one's play time.

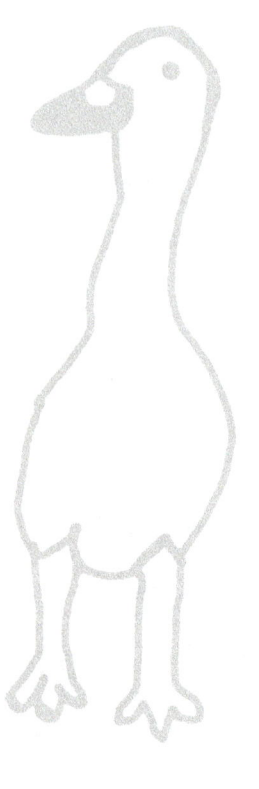

CHEWBEADS BABY SILICONE LINKS

INFANT ~ ~~TODDLER~~ ~ TINY TOTS ELITE

These silicone links are perfect for attaching your baby's toys and teethers to his stroller, high chair, or car seat. If you are weary of snatching up your baby's stuff from public floors, only to discover them on the ground again, you will be thankful for Chewbeads Baby Silicone Links.

They are super safe, not an around-the-neck choking hazard, and have a soft and flexible design. They come slightly open on the ends, but you can easily adjust the gap by squeezing the links together, or increase the gap a bit and let this be your baby's first experience of joining links together.

Chewbeads Baby Silicone Links have no BPA, no phthalates, no lead, no cadmium, and are easily cleaned with dish soap and water.

Scheduling
No need to schedule these - just use as desired.

LILLIPUTIENS WALTER DRAGON SQUEAKER

INFANT ~ ~~TODDLER~~ ~ TINY TOTS ELITE

A toy so soft that even a baby's touch can make it squeak? Yes! The surface-washable Walter Dragon Squeaker is not only easy for tiny hands to hold, but its super-pliable knit construction means that even the gentlest pressure will yield a peaceful squeak. Suitable for babies from birth, Walter Dragon Squeaker will visually delight baby with his different colors as well.

Scheduling
Move Walter back and forth in front of your infant to practice his visual tracking, and try it again while squeaking Walter to test his auditory tracking. As your baby grows, Walter can become an informal part of his play time.

Lilliputiens Romeo the Greedy Toad

INFANT ~ TODDLER ~ TINY TOTS ELITE

Romeo, a greedy toad, is not just an entertaining rattle, he is also an amusing way to increase your child's manipulative skills. His main body is made up of a pocket, in which his little fly friend dwells, attached with a pink fabric tongue.

Putting the fly in and out will develop your child's manipulation and orientation skills, which are necessary foundational visual motor skills later used to complete puzzles. Romeo the Greedy Toad is a great toy for early sensory play with a soft side, a corduroy side, shimmery wings on the fly, a crinkly paper-textured belly, and a bell rattle.

Our product testers loved the many features of Romeo, but found that the squeaker inside the fly isn't reliably functional. If yours works, that is another fun bonus feature! Romeo also has some handy pieces of fabric for carrying and teething, or to tie Romeo to baby's car seat or diaper bag.

Scheduling

Tie Romeo to your infant's car seat or add him to your selection of developmental toys for interactive playtime. Romeo doesn't need to be scheduled into every week, but make sure he is part of playtime a few times a month from infancy on.

Convergent & Divergent Thinking

Have you considered the necessity of incorporating both convergent and divergent thinking into your learning time? Experts recognize these as the two major types of brain challenges we all encounter.

What Is Convergent Thinking?

Convergent thinking generally involves finding a single best answer and is important in the study of math and science. Convergent thinking is the backbone of the majority of curricula and is crucial for future engineers, doctors, and even parents. Much of daily life is a series of determining right and wrong answers, and standardized tests favor the convergent thinker. But when we pursue only convergent-rich curricula, we miss the equally vital arena of divergent thinking.

Is Divergent Thinking Different?

Yes! Divergent thinking encourages your child's mind to explore many possible solutions, maybe even ideas that aren't necessarily apparent at first. It is in use when he discovers that there is more than one way to build a bridge with blocks, to animate a movie, or even simply to complete a doodle. Radically different from read-and-regurgitate textbooks, divergent activities are not only intellectually stimulating, but kids love them, too.

Make a Conscious Effort to Include Both This Year

At this age, both convergent and divergent thinking are naturally absorbed. Your child will creatively interact with the learning toys/tools in this kit, which is divergent thinking. As you read books together, you'll develop vocabulary, which is innately convergent (while a house might be called a house, home, or building, it is not called an airplane, flower, or cookie).

Practical Tips

Another smart way to implement both convergent and divergent learning at this age is as simple as varying what you ask. If you ask your toddler to make a tower identical to yours, you're asking him a question with only one right answer, so that's a convergent skill. To make it divergent, ask him to build you a tower as tall as yours, or one that uses the same colors. Now you've taken the same idea and added a divergent element. Just keep in mind that he needs both, and you'll be off and running!

Homeschooling Your Baby – Learning Styles

ORIGINALLY WRITTEN IN 1993, SHORTLY AFTER THE ADDITION OF PEARL, BABY #5.

Having a newborn has reminded us again of why we teach our children at home. Teaching your child does not begin with kindergarten curriculum, nor does it begin with a preschool program, or even with your baby's first step. Home education begins shortly after birth; it can begin with a cuddle.

Doesn't it seem that after you have your baby, everyone rushes to hold her? Our baby Pearl is no exception. She loves all the attention and seems to adore everyone who dotes on her. However, do not put her on your shoulder to cuddle. She will arch her back and let you know clearly that this is NOT where she belongs. Is she being difficult, acting spoiled, showing her sin nature already? If we had assumed that, then we would have missed a wonderful opportunity to nurture our baby.

Instead we recognized that Pearl is a visual baby, which means that she is wired to learn best by seeing the world around her. When people put Pearl on their shoulder, it limits Pearl's field of vision and thwarts her primary objective of seeing everything. In other words, they are incapacitating her learning agenda. But by holding her against themselves, face forward, she gets to see all that they see and she is not only contented, but is still able to fulfill her consuming passion to learn. Babies are born "learning machines," and learning is their first priority. But not all babies are visual babies.

Abel was an auditory baby, which means he learned best by hearing and experimenting with sound. As a baby, he loved to be cuddled on our shoulders, as close to our voice-box as possible. To soothe him we would merely hum and he would be so fascinated with the sound he would soon forget his discomfort.

Auditory babies are frustrated by a lot of noise because they want to sort out each sound, and the combination of sounds is overwhelming. When things are dull, auditory babies can create their own excitement with various chirps, coos, and patter. Even at this tender age they delight in listening to themselves "speak." Get used to the sound of their voice, because you are going to hear a lot of it!

A third type of baby scholar is the hands-on learner. Whereas the auditory or visual learner can satisfy their enthusiasm for investigating by sitting in your arms, the hands-on learner needs to be doing. Our Hope was such a learner and she would wiggle and squirm and move about just for the sheer pleasure it brought her. The saying "motion stops commotion" particularly suits this style of learner. She did not want to sit quietly, and had she been forced to, it would not have been best for her.

Bear in mind that we are not addressing areas of discipline here. There will undoubtedly be times when your wiggler needs to sit still for an exam, your auditory baby will need to be quiet during a meeting, and your visual baby may need to duck under a blanket to be nursed.

However, for the nurturing parent these times should be the exception and not the norm. The wiggler should not only be allowed to move about freely, she should be encouraged to do so. Again, thwarting this drive will impede the learning process.

The first step to teaching your baby at home is to let your baby teach you. What makes your baby laugh? All sorts of tickles will amuse your wiggler but leave your auditory baby sober. However, he will squeal with delight whenever Grandpa makes a funny sound. Your visual baby will love contorted faces and other forms of slapstick humor.

By doing your "homework" and studying your infant, you will discover what sort of learner he is. By determining what will soothe your baby and what amuses your baby, you will not only have one of your biggest clues as to what style of learner he is, you will be well on your way to nurturing a lifelong love of learning.

Homeschooling Your Baby – The Ideal Environment

ORIGINALLY WRITTEN IN 1993, SHORTLY AFTER THE ADDITION OF PEARL, BABY #5.

As a teaching mom, my first assignment is to study my baby and learn how she learns best. Keep in mind that many babies are a blend of styles, but all babies will have a decided preference.

When you are the parent of a visual baby, the road ahead of you will be fairly smooth. For whatever reason, nearly all canned curriculum is geared to the visual learner. Moreover, visual children who attend school have the greatest opportunity for success because most of their teachers will not only use a visual curriculum, but are visual learners themselves.

Visual babies study the details in the world around them. These are the babies that become the children that seem to teach themselves to read. Our Joy was reading words at 18 months and loving it! Because we know Pearl is likewise a visual baby, we will work to surround her with lots of visual stimulation. The easiest way for me to do this is through brightly colored picture books, but other ideas are posters, mirrors, toys, even a fish tank! My goal is to nourish the visual ability of my baby, to allow her to excel in an area in which she is very capable.

Our auditory babies have also picked up academic skills readily. The advantage they have is that nearly all my teaching is given orally first. This has given them at least one opportunity to master what is expected, and because auditory learners are so experienced at processing what they hear, they tend to be very successful.

We have found that our auditory babies are ideal candidates for music training and foreign languages. An environment with good music will begin a lifetime love of music. If we were bilingual, we would have capitalized on that skill while they were still infants. Instead, we did the next best thing and let them listen in while we played foreign language tapes.

A lesson we learned the hard way was to spend as much time as possible talking to our babies while there was still time. Before we knew it, they were talking, talking, talking. And that will continue throughout their childhood as they sing while they work, chant out their math facts, and yodel for the sheer pleasure of it. If it seems to you that their mouths are always in gear, keep in mind they truly do need to hear themselves think.

In the academic world, our hands-on babies are at a disadvantage. These children learn best by doing, but apart from some preschool/kindergarten activities, most curriculum is geared for visual learners. Our Hope needed an environment full of action. Hope was not content to sit and watch the action flow around her. As soon as possible, she hurled herself into that action. Hands-on babies learn by feeling and doing, so give them every opportunity to push, pull, squeeze, squish, dig, and dump. When Hope was a little older and involved in "hard-core academics" like puzzles and coloring, it amused us to no end to notice that she spent the entire morning standing at her child-size table. To ask her to sit to work on a puzzle would have bewildered her. How can you possibly do a puzzle without hopping, wiggling, or at the very least marching in place?! We could have forced her to sit quietly in a chair for schoolwork, but she would have been so engrossed in the labor of sitting still that there would have been no brain power left to solve puzzles. We saved the training of sitting still for when sitting still was the only goal.

Keep in mind that those wiggles are wired into your baby. When you think you just cannot clean up one more mess, tell yourself that to excel academically your baby needs as much active time as possible. I like to think that the more weary I am, the brighter my hands-on baby is becoming.

Once more, we are not addressing conduct here. We do not think we should abdicate our throne to a fifteen-pound tyrant. We do, however, have the intent of making our baby our course of intense study. What makes him sad and what makes him happy? What challenges him and what does he find boring? The more I know about my baby, the easier and more pleasant my career as a teaching parent will be.

TODDLER CONTAINMENT 101
SIX TIPS FOR SUCCESSFULLY INTEGRATING A TODDLER INTO YOUR HOME SCHOOL

As your baby becomes a toddler, you'll love his enthusiastic, loving, curious, confident, and innocent nature. However, to a home-educating parent, he will also be exhausting, impatient, loud, and unpredictable. So how can we incorporate him in with the older children in our education program without overwhelming them? Here are some ideas that have worked for us.

1) Keep It Fun!
Your goal is productive learning, and that can be accomplished through many fun methods. But if your child is not easily making the transition into being required to accomplish something, don't hesitate to bring out some motivators.

Why not make a chore board of all the different tasks you would like to accomplish in a week with your child, then let him choose which one he would like to do next. Flip over the finished task card (photos work great as cheap and easy chore cards) and you will move through all your goals for your child while also engaging him in the process. Even at this young age, you can begin to teach him how to structure his day independently.

Or, let your toddler earn a reward for finishing the tasks. For instance, have him pick out six tasks to do (using the picture cards again), and when the tasks are finished, he has earned the privilege of playing outside, listening to his music, or whatever else you find is motivating to him.

You can also use even more immediate rewards. When one child had difficulty tracing, we brought out fish crackers and set up a story where the fish needed to get home; as the child traced the line, the fish followed, and when she reached the end of each line she got to eat the fish.

2) Keep It Short
Keep the structured projects short and varied. Your toddler is much more likely to stay engaged for an hour if he has six to ten short projects, rather than spending all that time tracing letters. You can set him up for longer periods of time with activities he already enjoys such as water play, coloring, etc., but for structured learning, begin small.

3) Use All Your Child's Senses
Don't get tunnel vision and focus only on "workbook"-type tasks; there will be plenty of years for that later. Work to incorporate all your child's senses as you do different activities. The weekly checklist will help you be aware of what activities you've already done each week, so you don't accidently overlook anything.

4) Keep It Flexible
For a toddler, living is learning. New things, experiences, and skills to be learned surround your child. Structure is good, but don't forget that you can relax and enjoy the moment. If you don't get to puzzles this week, don't sweat it! If your toddler loves to paint, take time to encourage more painting. All of life is learning, so have fun and relax!

5) Incorporate Them When You Can

Most toddlers will be blissful if you let them participate in your art lessons. If you are using expensive supplies that they will destroy, try buying inexpensive sets that are just for them. They won't know the difference between deluxe and cheap paper, and a set of 24 markers for $3.00 will look like more fun to them than the $3.00-per-piece art markers! It helps to buy an art bin or caddie to store all their supplies in (markers, glue sticks, scissors, stickers, and so forth). Not only will this encourage orderliness, but toddlers love to sift and sort through their possessions.

6) Just for School Time

Our most obvious suggestion: Keep a box or a shelf of items that can only be used during the "big kids" school time. This can include items from this kit and/or other art supplies, workbooks, puzzles, blocks, and hands-on materials that are only brought out during this time. This distinction will add to their attractiveness and make the "learning hour" something your toddlers will anticipate every day!